Contemporary Diagnosis and Management of
Attention-Deficit/ Hyperactivity Disorder®

L. Eugene Arnold, MEd, MD

Professor Emeritus of Psychiatry

Ohio State University

Columbus, Ohio

Second Edition

D1446983

Published by Handbooks in Health Care Co.,
Newtown, Pennsylvania, USA

Acknowledgments

The author gratefully acknowledges invaluable critique of the manuscript, with many useful suggestions, by Mark L. Wolraich, MD, Professor of Pediatrics and Director of the Division of Child Development, Department of Pediatrics, Vanderbilt University, and by Richard Kern, MD, practicing pediatrician, Columbus, Ohio.

This book has been prepared and is presented as a service to the medical community. The information provided reflects the knowledge, experience, and personal opinions of the author, L. Eugene Arnold, MEd, MD, Professor Emeritus of Psychiatry, Ohio State University, Columbus, Ohio.

This book is not intended to replace or to be used as a substitute for the complete prescribing information prepared by each manufacturer for each drug. Because of possible variations in drug indications, in dosage information, in newly described toxicities, in drug/drug interactions, and in other items of importance, reference to such complete prescribing information is definitely recommended before any of the drugs discussed are used or prescribed.

International Standard Book Number: 1-884065-99-6

Library of Congress Catalog Card Number: 2001099314

Table of Contents

Chapter 1

Understanding ADHD: Description, Etiology, Course, and Complications

Attention-deficit/hyperactivity disorder (ADHD) is the most commonly diagnosed behavior disorder in North America, occurring in 3% to 8% of school children,[1] and in a smaller proportion of adults. ADHD is a chronic syndrome of age-inappropriate inattention, distractibility, impulsivity, and restless overactivity. It occurs more in males than in females by a ratio of 2:1 or 3:1 in nonclinical samples of children. The ratio is higher in clinical samples.[2] In adult-diagnosed samples, the sex ratio may approach equality.[2]

To educate and guide patients and their parents (or, in the case of adult patients, their significant others), clinicians must understand the definition and diagnosis of ADHD, its complications and comorbidity, and its etiology, pathogenesis, prevention, treatment, and palliation. Although important for any disorder, a thorough understanding becomes imperative for such a controversial issue. The very existence of ADHD, the validity of the diagnosis, has been repeatedly challenged by medical and lay critics, who often also condemn the most common and best-documented treatment, stimulant medication. This chapter summarizes some of the scientific facts, which—although not 100% conclusive—provide a reasonable basis of evidence for clinical decision-making.

Scientific Findings

In November 1998, the National Institutes of Health (NIH) held a 3-day consensus development conference[3,4] to summarize the scientific findings about ADHD and resolve some of the controversy. A panel of experts from outside the ADHD field, but with expertise in evaluating scientific and clinical evidence, listened to and read reviews of numerous topics by national ADHD experts and critics. One of the foremost critics of the concept and its treatment was an invited presenter, and other critics were given an opportunity to present their views and evidence supporting their criticisms. The panel drafted a summary report, which was presented to the assembled investigators, clinicians, and critics for comment, and was then revised. The conference concluded that:

1. The diagnosis is reliable, with roughly the same prevalence across cultures and continents when the same criteria are used.[5]
2. Although no simple biologic test is pathognomonic for the diagnosis (which is also true of many other mental disorders), converging lines of evidence suggest a biologic basis.[6]
3. Patients with stringently diagnosed ADHD have impairments across a wide range of functioning and settings.[7]
4. Comorbidities are common, and both ADHD and its comorbidities tend to be chronic.[8]
5. The disorder affects not only the patient, but also parents, siblings, peers, and school staff.[9]

These five descriptive conclusions are examined in this chapter after a historical divergence into the evolution of nomenclature and concept.

Name Changes Over the Decades

The syndrome has been known for more than 150 years, having been portrayed by the characters Fidgety Phil and Harry Who Looks in the Air in the 19th-century German book, *Strewelpeter*.[10] Other early names included Still's syndrome,[11] Strauss syndrome, and hyperkinetic impulse disorder or hyperkinetic syndrome, still preserved in the ICD-10 name for the disorder. ADHD was, for a time, considered a sequela of brain damage because most severe early cases were associated with biologic risks, such as von Economo's encephalitis, complicated gestation or delivery, head trauma, mental retardation, or seizures. When the same symptoms were found in children without such an explanatory history, the terms *minimal brain damage* or *minimal brain dysfunction* (MBD) came into vogue to indicate that clinicians suspected something was wrong with the brain, but could not demonstrate it by the tests then available. *Minimal cerebral dysfunction* was another term occasionally used, although little evidence suggested that any brain dysfunction was confined to the cerebrum rather than involving also the brain stem and cerebellum.

The original American Psychiatric Association Diagnostic and Statistical Manual (DSM) did not recognize the disorder. DSM-II (1970) used the term *hyperkinetic reaction*, implying that the syndrome was a reaction to some stress or pathogen (without evidence to support the imputed causality). Eventually, in the United States, the hybrid Greek-Latin term *hyperactive* crowded out the all-Greek *hyperkinetic*, with such names as hyperactive child syndrome. Until the 1970s, the naming had been based mainly on patients' obvious motor restlessness and, to some extent, impulsiveness, but experts were beginning to recognize that attention deficits were at least equally important, and perhaps more basic.

In 1980, DSM-III promoted the attention-deficit symptom to preeminent billing in the new name, *attention-deficit disorder*, with (ADDH) or without (ADD) hyperactivity.[12] DSM-IIIR resurrected hyperactivity with the name *attention-deficit hyperactivity disorder* (ADHD), attempting a unified concept by merging symptoms of attention deficit, hyperactivity, and impulsivity.[13] DSM-IV[14] (1994) preserved this name, but, based on data analyses, separated the inattention from hyperactivity-impulsivity, and established the diagnosis of subtypes with either set of symptoms. Although all the names listed roughly referred to the same syndrome (with epidemiologic overlap), they are not identical; each reflects a particular interest, observation, or causal thinking and may result in different estimates of prevalence.

The current name emphasizes attention deficits and overactivity, but impulsiveness (motor, verbal, and mental) may be the most central and unifying symptom. In ADHD, the lack of reflectiveness and executive function is compelling. Patients with the disorder act before they think, react before they think, speak before they think, and even think before they think, jumping to conclusions prematurely. The impulsiveness may be associated with impatient seeking of sensory input and other reinforcement; some evidence suggests that patients with ADHD do not find ordinary activities as inherently rewarding as do most age mates.

Diagnostic Criteria, Reliability, Validity, and Cross-Cultural Prevalence

Table 1-1 shows the current diagnostic criteria for ADHD, taken from DSM-IV. Note that there are two symptomatic dimensions developed from factor analyses of reported symptoms: inattentiveness, which includes distractibility, forgetfulness, disorganization, and failure to finish tasks or follow instructions; and hyperactivity-impulsivity, which includes impatience and excessive, nonreflective action and speech. These two dimensions make it possible to diagnose partial expressions—either inattentive type or hyperactive-impulsive type—in addition to the full-blown disorder, the combined type. The combined type, of course, meets criteria for both partially expressed types. It is the most common type in mental health clinics, but the partial types contribute to some of the higher prevalence estimates (prevalence varies according to whether only the combined type or all three types are counted). The partial types may predominate in some primary care clinics. An essential part of the criteria is the longevity of the behavior pattern, which must be present for at least 6 months and begin before age 7. The criteria also require that the symptoms cause some impairment in at least two settings: home, school, or peer functioning. ICD-10 criteria for hyperkinetic syndrome are similar but more stringent, approaching what DSM-IV considers ADHD combined type as reported by both parent and teacher.[15] Chapter 2 further examines diagnosis.

Both structured interviews and scalar instruments have demonstrated high test-retest and interrater reliability, and show validity in predicting independent clinician diagnosis, actometer readings, performance on neuropsychologic tests such as continuous performance test (CPT), objective systematic behavioral observations, underachievement, and later outcome.[15]

A review of epidemiologic studies from 15 countries on five continents over the past 15 years using a variety of definitions of the disorder found strong support for the cross-cultural validity of the syndrome despite prevalences ranging from 1% to 20% across cultures.[5] Although part of the difference in prevalence is undoubtedly attributable to setting and culture, Bird concluded that the "differences may be more a function of the diagnostic system . . . methods of ascertainment, and other methodological artifacts."[5] The syndrome itself shows high consistency across cultures and settings, for example, on factor analyses of diagnostic instruments, which repeatedly yielded two robust factors of inattention and hyperactivity-impul-

Table 1-1: Diagnostic Criteria for Attention-Deficit/Hyperactivity Disorder[14]

A. Either (1) or (2):

(1) Six (or more) of the following symptoms of **inattention** have persisted for at least 6 months to a degree that is maladaptive and inconsistent with developmental level:

Inattention

- (a) often fails to pay close attention to details or makes careless mistakes in schoolwork, work, or other activities

- (b) often has difficulty sustaining attention in tasks or play

- (c) often does not seem to listen when spoken to directly

- (d) often does not follow through on instructions and fails to finish schoolwork, chores, or duties in the workplace (not attributable to oppositional behavior or failure to understand instructions)

- (e) often has difficulty organizing tasks and activities

- (f) often avoids, dislikes, or is reluctant to engage in tasks that require sustained mental effort (such as schoolwork or homework)

- (g) often loses things necessary for tasks or activities (eg, toys, school assignments, pencils, books, or tools)

- (h) is often easily distracted by extraneous stimuli

- (i) is often forgetful in daily activities

(2) Six (or more) of the following symptoms of **hyperactivity/impulsivity** have persisted for at least 6 months to a degree that is maladaptive and inconsistent with developmental level:

Hyperactivity

   (a) often fidgets with hands or feet or squirms in seat

   (b) often leaves seat in classroom or in other situations where remaining seated is expected

   (c) often runs about or climbs excessively in inappropriate situations (in adolescents or adults, may be limited to subjective feelings of restlessness)

   (d) often has difficulty playing or engaging in leisure activities quietly

   (e) is often 'on the go' or often acts as if 'driven by a motor'

   (f) often talks excessively

Impulsivity

   (g) often blurts out answers before questions have been completed

   (h) often has difficulty awaiting turn

   (i) often interrupts or intrudes on others (eg, conversations or games)

B. Some hyperactive-impulsive or inattentive symptoms that caused impairment were present before 7 years of age.

C. Some impairment from the symptoms is present in two or more settings (eg, at school, work, home).

D. Clear evidence indicates clinically significant impairment in social, academic, or occupational functioning.

(continued on next page)

Table 1-1: Diagnostic Criteria for Attention-Deficit/Hyperactivity Disorder[14] (continued)

E. The symptoms do not occur exclusively during the course of a pervasive developmental disorder, schizophrenia, or other psychotic disorder, and are not better accounted for by another mental disorder (eg, mood disorder, anxiety disorder, dissociative disorder, or a personality disorder).

Code based on type:

314.01 Attention-Deficit/Hyperactivity Disorder, Combined Type: if both criteria Al and A2 are met for the past 6 months

314.00 Attention-Deficit/Hyperactivity Disorder, Predominantly Inattentive Type: if criterion Al is met but criterion A2 is not met for the past 6 months

314.01 Attention-Deficit/Hyperactivity Disorder, Predominantly Hyperactive-Impulsive Type: if criterion A2 is met but criterion Al is not met for the past 6 months

Coding note: For individuals (especially adolescents and adults) who have symptoms that no longer meet full criteria, *In Partial Remission* should be specified.

314.9 Attention-Deficit/Hyperactivity Disorder, Not Otherwise Specified: This category is for disorders with prominent symptoms of inattention or hyperactivity-impulsivity that do not meet criteria for Attention-Deficit/Hyperactivity Disorder.

Reprinted with permission from *Diagnostic and Statistical Manual of Mental Disorders, 4th ed (DSM-IV)*. Copyright 1994, American Psychiatric Association.

sivity. Another example is the finding that a Chinese sample had the same neuropsychologic test deficits, actometer readings, and history of biologic risk factors and developmental delays as reported in Western samples.[5] Consequently, despite some informant differences by culture, a stringent definition yields reasonably consistent prevalence across cultures. Reviewing all the available data, Bird estimated the worldwide prevalence of the DSM-IV diagnosis at 4% to 5% in middle childhood.[5]

Biologic Basis and Etiology of ADHD

Although causation and pathogenesis have not been completely defined, converging lines of evidence make a convincing case for a biologic basis in most cases. One of the best documented and pervasive causes is a genetic diathesis for many, perhaps most, cases. Many family studies, twin studies, and adoption studies have consistently reported high heritability,[6] usually above 0.5. Although specific genetic mechanisms have not been definitively documented, two dopamine genes have been reported to be associated with the disorder: the dopamine transporter gene (DAT1) and the D4 dopamine receptor gene (DRD4). Preliminary hypotheses are that: (1) the 10-repeat allele of DAT1 on chromosome 5p15.3 results in too-rapid reuptake of dopamine, and (2) the 7-repeat allele of DRD4 on chromosome 11p15.5 results in dopamine receptor hyposensitivity.[6] Both of these hypotheses are compatible with the dopamine-deficiency hypothesis of pathogenesis, which was suggested by the fact that most drugs that are beneficial for the disorder enhance dopamine neurotransmission.[6] However, the two genes so far identified do not appear to account for the degree of heritability found in family, adoptive, and twin studies, and the variability appears too great to use them as clinical diagnostic markers.

Four independent groups of investigators using anatomic magnetic resonance imaging (MRI) have found that ADHD brains are smaller than controls in the frontal areas (especially right), basal ganglia (especially caudate nucleus), and cerebellar vermis. Such findings are compatible with neuropsychologic tests showing impairment of executive function (planning, inhibition of impulse, voluntary direction of attention) subserved by the frontal lobes and attentional systems subserved by basal ganglia. Unfortunately, other brain imaging strategies, such as positron emission tomography (PET), have not yielded the same results, so it is not yet possible to draw any firm conclusions from functional studies, such as PET, single-proton emission tomography (SPECT), computerized EEG brain mapping, and functional MRI.[6]

Besides genetic diathesis, numerous environmental and indirect pathophysiologic etiologies are reportedly associated with inattention and hyperactivity in animals or humans, at least in small populations.[16] In addition to the encephalitis, birth trauma, cranial anomalies, head injuries, fragile X, and fetal alcohol syndrome associated with the earliest recognition of the syndrome, more recent reports implicate heavy metal poisoning, zinc and other mineral deficiency, specific essential fatty acid deficiency, specific food component sensitivities/allergies, thyroid abnormality, and pediatric autoimmune disorder associated with group A β-hemolytic streptococcal infection.[17-19] Probably no one of these is important in more than a small minority of ADHD cases, and most are found in only single-digit percentages (eg, thyroid abnormality may be as low as 2%). However, in the aggregate, these problems appear to complicate a considerable proportion of cases. Furthermore, they may be compatible with the genetic and brain imaging findings. For example, some of the heritability may result from inheritance of immune disorder or thyroid dysfunction; heavy metal poisoning, viral exposure, or nutritional deficiency might impair growth of specific brain regions; or deficiency of zinc, necessary for optimal dopamine function, might further stress a borderline DRD4 status.[16]

As with most neuropsychiatric disorders, stress aggravates the symptoms. Overwhelming stress resulting in posttraumatic stress disorder or major depression can even mimic many symptoms of ADHD. Hyperactivity has been reported as a sequela of maternal deprivation.

In summary, the development of clinical symptoms likely results from interaction of genetic diathesis with environment, both physical/chemical and psychosocial. Figure 1-1 depicts a hydraulic parfait model of the additive effect of various etiologies and complications in producing clinical symptoms. Neutralizing some of the etiology on any layer might shrink the total level enough to stop symptom spill and impairment. Therefore, a physician should make sure a treatable etiology is not missed in a given case. Figure 1-2 depicts the accumulation of symptoms that trigger a diagnosis. Diagnosis, once launched, can be as difficult to retrieve as a bullet, and can induce a qualitative change in the way the patient views himself or herself and is viewed by parents, teachers, and peers.

Impairments From ADHD

Impairments in executive function underlie most of the other domains of impairment. Executive function is the ability to organize, plan, attend to, and remember relevant details and instructions, screen out irrelevant distractions, prioritize options, marshal resources, inhibit or delay competing or otherwise inappropriate action, and carry a plan through to completion. The inverse relationship to core ADHD symptoms is obvious. In fact, ADHD is often characterized as a disorder of executive function.

The deficits in attention, impulse control, and activity modulation cause secondary impairments in many domains of function. These occur not only in clinical samples, where impairment is expected, but also in epidemiologic samples, and even when diagnosis is made without requiring the impairment criterion shown in Table 1-1, dem-

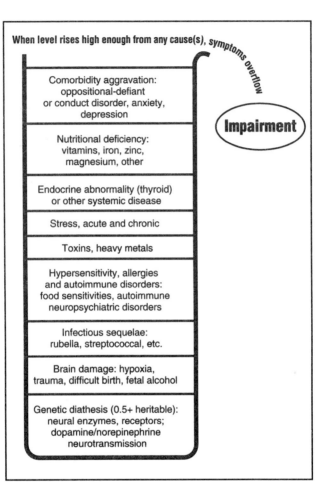

Figure 1-1: *Hydraulic parfait showing additive effect of possible causes of ADHD. No single layer of the parfait is necessary in an individual case. In fact, some etiologies are not present in most cases. A sufficiently thick layer of one etiology or an accumulated level from several etiologies can make the level spill over into impairing clinical symptoms. Adapted with permission from Arnold.*[20]

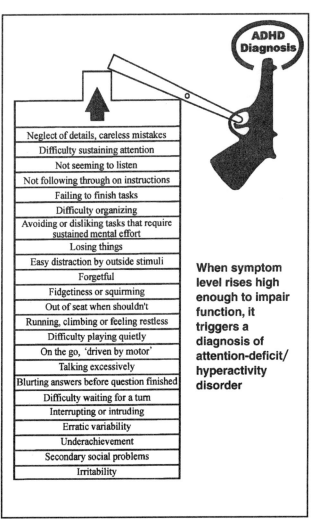

Neglect of details, careless mistakes
Difficulty sustaining attention
Not seeming to listen
Not following through on instructions
Failing to finish tasks
Difficulty organizing
Avoiding or disliking tasks that require sustained mental effort
Losing things
Easy distraction by outside stimuli
Forgetful
Fidgetiness or squirming
Out of seat when shouldn't
Running, climbing or feeling restless
Difficulty playing quietly
On the go, 'driven by motor'
Talking excessively
Blurting answers before question finished
Difficulty waiting for a turn
Interrupting or intruding
Erratic variability
Underachievement
Secondary social problems
Irritability

ADHD Diagnosis

When symptom level rises high enough to impair function, it triggers a diagnosis of attention-deficit/ hyperactivity disorder

Figure 1-2: Dynamics of diagnosis. When enough symptoms accumulate with sufficient impairment, the symptom pressure triggers a diagnosis. Adapted and used with permission from Arnold.[20]

onstrating that it is not mere circularity from the DSM-IV diagnostic criteria. Moreover, impairments are chronic, persisting into adulthood.[8] The description below is based mainly on the more severe cases found in mental health samples; primary care cases include the less severe end of the impairment spectrum.

One of the most important domains of impairment concerns social skills and peer status.[7,8] The intrusiveness and sometimes aggression resulting from hyperactivity and impulsiveness, coupled with inattentiveness to social cues, lead to difficulty socializing appropriately. Most children with ADHD have difficulty in keeping friends (they rapidly 'wear them out'), and some have trouble making friends. They may claim to have 'lots' of friends, but really mean acquaintances. In fact, children with ADHD have a high rate of peer rejection, probably resulting from their impaired social skills. This impairment is ominous, because peer rejection is one of the best predictors of delinquency, dropout, and adult maladjustment.[7]

Another domain of ADHD-caused impairment is academic achievement and, especially, academic performance. Achievement is what is actually learned, as measured by individual achievement tests; academic performance or productivity is quantity and quality of schoolwork, on which grades depend. Youngsters with ADHD typically underperform academically and may underachieve even if they do not have comorbid learning disorder, as 20% to 25% do. The combination of poor attention, distractibility, and disorganization understandably puts such a child at a disadvantage in school, and may lead to progressively more problems in secondary schools, which require more self-organizational skills. Attention problems seem particularly damaging for mathematical achievement and performance, where unflagging attention to detail is essential. Follow-up studies show that those diagnosed with ADHD completed less education than control subjects.[21]

The parent-child relationship also suffers. Even before parental disappointment in school and household chore performance develops, parents may have been stressed by their preschooler's overactive impulsiveness. As one parent described it, these are often *high-maintenance children.* The need for treatment or other special services may further tax the parents' resources. Stressed parents lead to stressed family relations and stressed children. In desperation, parents often drift into aversive or otherwise discordant parenting practices, and sometimes even child abuse. High rates of marital discord and divorce occur among couples with ADHD children.[8] Divorce, of course, adds to stress for both parents and child. Because any disorder, including ADHD, is aggravated by stress, a vicious circle often develops in which the child's symptoms fuel family stress, and family stress aggravates the child's symptoms.[7]

The difficulties succeeding with peers, at school, and at home can lead to impairments of self-esteem. However, many persons with ADHD may deny or defend against perceived deficits by presenting with overconfidence or bravado.

ADHD can even impair a patient's physical health. Research suggests a higher rate of accidents in ADHD patients than in control groups,[7,8] including a higher rate of automobile accidents among adolescent drivers with ADHD compared with other adolescents. Accidental head injury caused by inattention and hyperactive impulsivity can result in causal circularity because brain injury can cause or aggravate ADHD symptoms. Another area of causal circularity is the overlap between ADHD and child abuse. Children with ADHD 'invite' abuse, and head injuries from abuse can cause or aggravate ADHD.

Compared with controls, adults who had an ADHD diagnosis in childhood have lower-status jobs, more difficulty completing tasks, and higher rates of quitting and being laid off.[21] They also had lower social skills in simulated job interviews and in heterosexual interactions. Compared with controls, adults with clinically diagnosed ADHD also have higher rates of marital problems, separation, and divorce. Moreover, they appear impaired in child-rearing strategies and ability to co-parent.[21] The latter is particularly ominous because their children have a high risk for ADHD themselves and need superior parenting.

Comorbidities and Chronic Developmental Course

The symptoms of ADHD, especially overactivity, tend to become less obvious with maturity, but in many, perhaps in most cases, do not resolve completely. (See also Chapter 9 and Figure 9-1.) Normal individuals develop better impulse control, motor restfulness, and ability to focus and attend during successive developmental stages into young adulthood; so do patients with ADHD. However, they tend to remain at some disadvantage to age peers, especially for attentional skills and reflectiveness. Of young children diagnosed in mental health settings, between two thirds and three quarters continue to meet diagnostic criteria into early adolescence, and between one third and one half continue to meet criteria in late adolescence. Additional significant proportions continue to have troublesome symptoms below the diagnostic threshold. The reported persistence into adulthood depends on whether investigators depended on self-report (3% to 8%) or other informants (25% to 68%).[8]

The common comorbidities of ADHD also tend to change over the course of development. For example, about half of children with ADHD in mental health settings also have *oppositional-defiant disorder (ODD)*, *conduct disorder (CD)*, or both in succession. The rate in primary care settings is lower but still substantial. ODD is a testy, argumentative, spiteful, demanding, or negativistic attitude with disobedience, frequent tantrums, passive-aggressiveness, and sometimes aggression. It often progresses to CD, which has some of the same features as ODD, but adds more serious antisocial behavior, such as bullying, fighting with weapons, cruelty, truancy, habitual lying, extortion, forced sex, breaking and entering, arson, vandalism, shoplifting, and forgery. By adolescence, 20% to 50% of children with ADHD from mental health samples develop CD, and up to 25% may progress (after age 18) to adult antisocial personality.[8] Because aggression (verbal and physical) is so prominent in ODD and CD, and because this comorbidity is so common with ADHD, many people associate aggression with ADHD. Therefore, it is important to understand that aggression is not a diagnostic criterion for ADHD, and its prominent presence suggests ODD or CD. Some experts, especially in Europe, consider ADHD plus ODD/CD a separate subtype of ADHD, or even a separate disorder.

Between 25% and 35% of clinical samples of children with ADHD also have a diagnosable *anxiety disorder* beyond simple phobia. Because symptoms somewhat overlap (autonomic instability, concentration problems), the two disorders have an additive effect on some diagnostic instruments. The comorbid presence of anxiety has implications for treatment that are addressed later.

Comorbid *mood disorders* exist, probably at rates higher than expected by chance, but their prevalence is a matter of controversy. Biederman et al[22] reported a 23% rate of comorbid bipolar (manic-depressive) disorder among ADHD patients, but other investigators cannot replicate this. Comorbid depression is often diagnosed, but we do not know how much of this is secondary to the frustration and failure attendant to the ADHD symptoms and how much of it is primary coincident depression. Comorbid major depression appears to increase with age, especially among females with ADHD. One follow-up study found a major-depression rate of 28% in the 20 to 30 age range.[7] It is often associated with CD or subsequent antisocial personality. Comorbid depression has treatment implications.

The comorbid CD and later antisocial personality (diagnosable only after age 18) bring another common comorbidity: *substance abuse* in adolescence and adulthood. The reported risk of substance abuse or dependence by adulthood ranges from 10% to 37%.[8] The most common substances abused are alcohol, nicotine, and marijuana, but other drugs may also be involved. Some of this drug use may be attempted self-medication, especially the nicotine. Interestingly, there does not seem to be any special predilection to abuse stimulant medications.

Tourette's disorder consists of chronic, multiple phonic and motor tics (purposeless, spasmodic, stereotyped, repeated contractions of a muscle group). Although not common in ADHD, it is much less common in the general population. Approximately half of all Tourette's cases also have ADHD, but only about 2% of ADHD cases also have Tourette's. When the two conditions occur together, ADHD usually precedes Tourette's by 2 to 4 years, so ADHD must be considered a risk factor for Tourette's. Tourette's, when it occurs, is chronic, with some waxing and waning over time. It also has treatment implications.

Learning disorder is academic achievement substantially below ability level not explained by poor schooling or other lack of opportunity or incentive. It may be subject-specific (eg, reading or arithmetic disorder) or pervade several domains of academic function, in which case each specific disorder is diagnosed. About 20% to 25% of children with ADHD (higher for inattentive type) have learning disorder beyond the problems of inattention. This is one of the few mental disorders for which the diagnosis requires formal psychological testing; failing grades alone do not make the diagnosis because academic underperformance could arise from attention problems. (Academic performance is the production of school work on exams and projects that earn grades; achievement is what the child has learned.) Learning disorders are often associated with communication (language) disorders, which may also require formal testing to confirm the diagnosis.

Impact on Others Besides the Patient

Besides the stress on parents, including higher marital stress and divorce rates, the siblings of ADHD patients also suffer. Children with ADHD drain family resources (emotional, attentional, temporal, and financial). Younger siblings may suffer from the reputation their hyperactive forerunner has earned at school and in the neighborhood— important points for pediatricians and family practitioners. Peers, as well as siblings, may find their activities disrupted by the patient's intrusiveness, impulsiveness, and impatience. Teammates may find their game lost by the patient's inattentiveness. Coaches may struggle to keep the patient's attention on the rules of the game or strategic instruction. In adulthood, employers, mates, and bridge partners may be similarly affected.

The child's symptoms may beleaguer teachers even more than parents and coaches, because the demands of school (be still, pay attention, complete work) tend to bring out the symptoms in full flower. Need for disciplinary action and counseling may require irritatingly large amounts of time and effort from the principal, vice principal, or school counselor. Regular classes may not meet the needs of many ADHD children. Nearly 1 million American children with ADHD are in special educational programs on at least a part-time basis, at a cost of more than $3 billion annually,[9] so that taxpayers, too, are affected.

Quantitative Disorder, Strengths, and Evolutionary Background

The symptoms or deficits of ADHD are neither pathognomonic nor qualitatively different from variations of traits or abilities found in all persons. Everyone has some ability to voluntarily direct attention and yet be distracted by salient stimuli; and everyone has a preferred activity level with some reflex reactivity. The impairment (and hence disorder) arises from the consistent excess of activity, distractibility, and impulsive reactivity. This is analogous to hypertension, in which some blood pressure is normal, but too much (or too little) is impairing or pathologic. The patient with hypertension and the patient with ADHD may both be said to have too much of a good thing.

Strong evidence for a genetic factor in the etiology of ADHD and the fact that recognition of ADHD as a problem has soared with the information revolution have induced several authors[4,16,23] to hypothesize evolutionary explanations for the disorder. Human technology, social institutions, and lifestyles have evolved much faster than biology, so that traits that were advantageous in a previous setting might lose their value or even become handicaps in a different setting. According to this hypothesis, attending school, reading and ciphering, and office work are relatively new and 'unnatural' for humans in the evolutionary perspective. In a hunter-gatherer society, and even in primitive agricultural societies with a need for an informal militia against marauders, there may have been an advantage for some individuals to be reactive rather than reflective, to be easily distracted by a slight motion or sound in the periphery, and to respond reflexively, even impulsively. In a setting where such abilities are prized, the reactive end of the reactive-reflective spectrum would be advantageous, whereas in a setting where reflection is prized (eg, school, office, some games), the opposite end of the spectrum is advantageous. In a sense, inattentiveness is a wealth of distractibility and reflectiveness is a deficit of impulsive reactivity. In this perspective, individuals with ADHD may have an evolved talent for which the social value has largely attenuated. Nevertheless, with some thought, they may still be able to find a niche where their abilities are put to good use. This concept can be useful in destigmatizing the diagnosis of ADHD and in counseling the patient.

References

1. Richters JE, Arnold LE, Jensen PS, et al: The NIMH collaborative multisite multimodal treatment study of children with ADHD (MTA): I. Background & rationale. *J Am Acad Child Adolesc Psychiatry* 1995;34:987-1000.

2. Arnold LE: Sex differences in ADHD: conference summary. *J Abnorm Child Psychol* 1996;24:555-569.

3. National Institutes of Mental Health. *Program and Abstracts of NIH Consensus Development Conference on Diagnosis and Treatment of ADHD*. Bethesda, MD, NIH, 1998.

4. Jensen PS, Cooper J, eds. *Diagnosis and Treatment of ADHD: An Evidence-Based Approach*. Washington, DC, American Psychological Press, 2001. In press.

5. Bird H: The prevalence and cross-cultural validity of attention-deficit hyperactivity disorder. *Abstracts of NIH Consensus Development Conference on Diagnosis and Treatment of ADHD*. Bethesda, MD, NIH, 1998.

6. Swanson JM, Castellanos FX: Biological bases of attention-deficit/hyperactivity disorder: neuroanatomy, genetics, and pathophysiology. *Abstracts of NIH Consensus Development Conference on Diagnosis and Treatment of ADHD*. Bethesda, MD, NIH, 1998.

7. Hinshaw SP: Impairment: childhood and adolescence. *Abstracts of NIH Consensus Development Conference on Diagnosis and Treatment of ADHD*. Bethesda, MD, NIH, 1998.

8. Barkley RA: ADHD: long-term course, adult outcome, and comorbid disorders. *Abstracts of NIH Consensus Development Conference on Diagnosis and Treatment of ADHD*. Bethesda, MD, NIH, 1998.

9. Forness SR: The impact of ADHD on school systems. *Abstracts of NIH Consensus Development Conference on Diagnosis and Treatment of ADHD*. Bethesda, MD, NIH, 1998.

10. Hoffman H: *Strewelpeter (Slovenly Peter); or, Cheerful Stories and Funny Pictures for Good Little Folks*. Translated by Mark Twain from 1845 book. Philadelphia, Porter & Coates, 1935.

11. Still G: Some abnormal psychical conditions in children. *Lancet* 1902;1:1008-1012, 1077-1082, 1163-1168.

12. American Psychiatric Association, Committee on Nomenclature and Statistics. *Diagnostic and Statistical Manual of Mental Disorders 3rd Ed* (DSM-III). Washington, DC, American Psychiatric Association, 1980.

13. American Psychiatric Association, Committee on Nomenclature and Statistics. *Diagnostic and Statistical Manual of Mental Disorders 3rd Ed.*-Revised (DSM-IIIR). Washington, DC, American Psychiatric Association, 1987.

14. American Psychiatric Association. *Diagnostic and Statistical Manual of Mental Disorders, 4th ed* (DSM-IV). Washington, DC, American Psychiatric Association, 1994.

15. Lahey BB, Willcut EG: *Abstracts of NIH Consensus Development Conference on Diagnosis and Treatment of ADHD*. Bethesda, MD, NIH, 1998

16. Arnold LE, Jensen PS: Attention deficit hyperactivity disorder. In: Kaplan H, Sadock B, eds. *Comprehensive Textbook of Psychiatry*. Baltimore, Williams & Wilkins, 1995.

17. Arnold LE: Treatment alternatives for ADHD. *Abstracts of NIH Consensus Development Conference on Diagnosis and Treatment of ADHD*. Bethesda, MD, NIH, 1998.

18. Arnold LE: Treatment alternatives for ADHD. *J Attention Disord* 1999;3:30-48.

19. Arnold LE: Treatment alternatives for ADHD. Abstracts of NIH Consensus Development Conference on Diagnosis and Treatment of ADHD. In: Jensen P, Cooper, J, eds. *Diagnosis and Treatment of ADHD: an Evidence-based Approach.* Washington, DC, APPI. In press.

20. Arnold LE: Minimal brain dysfunction: a hydraulic parfait model. *Diseases of the Nervous System.* 37(4), 171-173, ©1976, Physicians Postgraduate Press.

21. Johnston C: The impact of attention-deficit/hyperactivity disorder on social and vocational functioning in adults. *Abstracts of NIH Consensus Development Conference on Diagnosis and Treatment of ADHD*. Bethesda, MD, NIH, 1998.

22. Biederman J, Faraone S, Mick E, et al: Attention-deficit hyperactivity disorder and juvenile mania: an overlooked comorbidity? *J Am Acad Child Adolesc Psychiatry* 1996;35:997-1008.

23. Jensen PS, Mrazek D, Knapp PK, et al: Evolution and revolution in child psychiatry: ADHD as a disorder of adaptation. *J Am Acad Child Adolesc Psychiatry* 1997;36:1672-1679.

Review Quiz

This quiz reinforces the key clinical points made in Chapter 1, points all physicians should understand.

True-False:

1. The so-called ADHD symptoms are not qualitatively different from normal behavior.
2. Evidence for ADHD has been found in 15 countries on five continents.
3. The prevalence rate of ADHD depends on the definition used.
4. ADHD usually impairs only academic performance.
5. Patients with ADHD, though underachieving as children, catch up with peers in young adulthood in educational attainment and career success.
6. ADHD is an unreliable diagnosis.
7. Environmental etiologies, such as food sensitivities, heavy metal toxicity, and nutritional deficiency, account for the bulk of ADHD symptoms.
8. The primary symptoms of ADHD attenuate with age.
9. Up to half of clinical cases of ADHD also have oppositional-defiant disorder or conduct disorder.
10. About 10% of ADHD cases also have anxiety or depression.
11. ADHD often precedes Tourette's disorder.
12. Heritability of ADHD is about 0.1.
13. In many patients, ADHD has far-reaching and pervasive impairments in multiple domains of function.
14. Untreated ADHD can be hazardous to the patient's health and safety.
15. Excess inattentiveness, distractibility, hyperactivity, and impulsive aggression are essential features of ADHD.

Multiple Choice:

16. For ADHD:
    a. there are pathognomonic neurologic and brain scan abnormalities
    b. there is ample evidence of a biologic basis
    c. there is convergent family-genetic and brain imaging evidence for a biologic basis
    d. there is no evidence for a biologic basis
    e. none of the above

17. ADHD:
    a. is usually outgrown by adulthood
    b. progresses with age
    c. continues unchanged through life as a chronic disorder
    d. varies in life course from one patient to another
    e. has no data base relevant to developmental course

Answer Key:

1. True. Like hypertension and hypotension, ADHD symptoms are pathologic excesses or deficits of normal physiology/behavior. The pathology is in the quantity, not the quality.

2. True.

3. True. Prevalence can be manipulated, among other ways, by setting different thresholds for pathologic number and severity of symptoms, just as prevalence of hypertension can be manipulated by setting different thresholds of pathology for blood pressure.

4. False. While it may impair academic performance more than achievement, it may impair many domains of function, at school, home, work, play, with peers, etc.

5. False. Many continue to lag behind age peers in adulthood.

6. False. Despite such problems as low correlations between parent and teacher ratings, there is reasonable test/retest reliability and reliability between experienced diagnosticians.

7. False.

8. True, but secondary symptoms and comorbidities often worsen with age.

9. True.

10. False. One quarter to one third have anxiety disorder.

11. True.

12. False. Heritability is about 0.5 to 0.8.

13. True.

14. True. Both children and adolescents with ADHD are more accident-prone than age peers and more vulnerable to substance abuse.

15. False. The first three are, and impulsivity is, but aggression is not a diagnostic criterion for ADHD.

16. C.

17. D. A few patients seem to outgrow the problem and many improve with time, but others continue to have serious impairment, and a few deteriorate, with additional complications and comorbidity, developing into serious adult pathology.

Chapter 2

Evaluation and Diagnosis

When a patient presents with complaints of inattention, disorganization, overactivity, restlessness, or impulsiveness, the clinician must resolve two key questions in the diagnostic evaluation:

(1) Does the patient have a disorder requiring treatment, or are the problems just part of the normal travails of life and normal growth and development—or intermediately, is there a subdiagnostic problem requiring intervention?

(2) If the patient does have a clinical disorder, is it ADHD, or would another diagnosis better explain the problems?

Of course, the DSM-IV diagnostic criteria for ADHD[1] in Table 1-1 of Chapter 1 require that the symptoms cause impairment to constitute a disorder. Those criteria are endorsed by the American Academy of Pediatrics (AAP) guideline,[2] as well as by the American Psychiatric Association.[1]

Basis of Evaluation

In approaching the evaluation, it is important to note that the diagnosis of ADHD is made by *history*, not by office observation. ADHD is a chronic pattern of behavior and function, and, therefore, cannot be assessed from a brief time sample, but must be corroborated by history. All symptoms of ADHD are only quantitative, ie, they are abnormal only in degree, by their persistence or repetition over time, as observed by caregivers, and may temporarily subside to normal levels in unusual situations, such as in a doctor's office. Because patients with ADHD (especially children) are sometimes poorly aware of their own problems, and are, therefore, frequently inaccurate reporters, the history should be collected not only from the patient, but also (even mainly) from parents, teachers, other caregivers, or, in the case of adults, significant others. One of the key points in the AAP guideline for diagnosing ADHD is the importance of obtaining information from more than one setting.[2]

The main values of physical and mental status examinations and laboratory tests are to rule out mimicking disorders, to detect a treatable etiology when possible, and to diagnose comorbidities, including developmental coordination disorder. ADHD itself is a phenomenologic diagnosis that says nothing about etiology. It may have various causes, some of which are directly treatable.

Applying the Diagnostic Criteria

Despite their reliability and improvement over previous versions, the DSM-IV diagnostic criteria shown in Table 1-1 (Chapter 1) entail several problems, especially as applied in primary care settings. The criteria were developed for elementary-school children and may require too many symptoms for adolescents and adults, who may 'lose' a few symptoms as they mature but still remain impaired. Just as normal individuals exhibit less impulsiveness and distractibility as they mature, persons with ADHD may also have fewer such diagnostic features with maturation, while still having more symptoms compared to age peers (see Chapter 9, Figure 9-1). Eventually, there may be age 'norms' for diagnosis.

Another shortfall of the diagnostic criteria is the ambiguity of the term *often* in the symptom list (Chapter 1, Table 1-1). Clearly, the intent is that the symptom must occur more frequently than in developmental peers. But how much more often? The answer falls to the judgment of the diagnostician and of the parents and teachers who provide information. That judgment is not so difficult in a tertiary care setting, where the decision is focused more on which disorder the patient has. The patient is not likely to progress to a specialist unless the *often* criterion is met and there really is a disorder. However, accurate judgment is difficult in the primary care setting, where the critical decision is determining whether there is a disorder or a problem deserving attention, or merely a variation of normal.

The fact that ADHD symptoms represent extremes of normal traits and abilities allows for subdiagnostic problems and variations of normal, as well as diagnosable disorders. In analogy with hypertension, if the pathologic level is set at > 90 mm Hg diastolic for adults, then consistent, repeated 94 diastolic would be considered diagnosable disorder; persistent 88 diastolic might be a blood pressure 'problem' (deserving some clinical attention even if not diagnosed); and 82 diastolic a variation of normal (needing no intervention). Accordingly, the *Diagnostic and Statistical Manual for Primary Care* (Wolraich et al, 1996) lists three possible gradations: 'variation' (V65), in which trends or fragments of ADHD symptoms can be discerned in the patient's behavior, but without impairment beyond mild nuisance to caregivers; 'behavior problem' (V40), in which there is impairment from ADHD symptoms without meeting diagnostic criteria (also diagnosable as 314.9 ADHD NOS); and 'disorder,' in which all diagnostic criteria for ADHD are met, including impairment in two or more settings.[3]

A primary care physician especially, but also any clinician, needs an easy, systematic way of quantifying the symptoms. One way to do this is to enlist the help of parents, teachers, babysitters, coaches, or significant others in filling out normed rating scales. For children, teachers are especially valuable raters because they can compare the patient to a large group of age peers. Figure 2-1 is the SNAP-IV (ADHD checklist), which includes the DSM-IV symptoms in a scale with a 0 to 3 rating from 'not at all' to 'very much.' The form shown is for children, but it can be adapted for adults. Alternate descriptors for the 4-point scale have been proposed: 'never,' 'sometimes,' 'often,' and 'very often.'[4] Generally, a symptom should not be counted if it is scored 0 or 1 ('just a little' or 'sometimes'); only those scored 2 ('quite a bit' or 'often') or 3 ('very much' or 'very often') should be counted.

Children who are diagnosed by experts as having ADHD, combined type, average an item mean of about 2 (or more) on the entire SNAP scale, but a valid diagnosis is possible with a lower mean if 6 of the 9 symptoms are present in one cluster. Parents and teachers often disagree on specific-item ratings of the same child because they observe in different settings and at different times, when circumstances elicit different symptoms. Therefore, the clinician can combine symptoms from parent and teacher scales to total the 6 of 9 required for each subtype diagnosis. Adults may have significant pathology with fewer symptoms. However, some impairing symptoms must be present in two or more settings for diagnosis—and the symptoms alone do not make the diagnosis without impairment of function, chronicity (≥ 6 months, dating from before age 7), and ruling out of mimicking disorders.

Another, more global approach that can be combined with the SNAP is the worksheet shown in Figure 2-2, which provides a convenient way to take notes about the history during patient and family interviews. The matrix serves as a reminder to cover important general areas. In using it, the clinician first asks about functioning in each of four areas (top row). If there is no problem, the rest of that column can be ignored. If there are problems, getting details will allow the appropriate sections of the respective column to be completed. The key to filling in the columns is impairment of function: eg, does inattention in-

Figure 2-1: SNAP-IV (DSM-IV ADHD Symptom Checklist)

Child's name_____Date___/___/___

Filled out by:_____Relationship:_____

Please check for each behavior whether it describes this child not at all, just a little, quite a bit, or very much in comparison to normal children of the same age and intelligence.

Behaviors

1.	Often neglects details or makes careless mistakes in schoolwork or tasks
2.	Often has difficulty sustaining attention in tasks or play
3.	Often does not seem to listen when spoken to
4.	Often does not follow through on instructions; fails to finish schoolwork, chores, or duties
5.	Often has difficulty organizing tasks and activities
6.	Often avoids, dislikes, or engages reluctantly in tasks that require sustained mental effort
7.	Often loses things necessary for tasks/activities
8.	Often easily distracted by outside stimuli
9.	Often forgetful in daily activities
10.	Often fidgets with hands or feet, or squirms
11.	Often leaves seat in situations in which remaining seated is expected
12.	Often runs or climbs excessively in situations where not appropriate (or for adolescents/adults, feels restless)

	Not at All	Just a Little	Quite a Bit	Very Much

(continued on next page)

**Figure 2-1: SNAP-IV (DSM-IV ADHD
Symptom Checklist)** *(continued)*

Behaviors

13. Often has difficulty playing or engaging in leisure
    activities quietly

14. Often 'on the go' or acts as if 'driven by a motor'

15. Often talks excessively

16. Often blurts out answers before questions are
    completed

17. Often has difficulty waiting for a turn

18. Often interrupts or intrudes on others
    (conversations, games)

When did these behaviors first start?

Adapted with permission from James M. Swanson, PhD,
previously appeared in: Swanson JM: *School-Based
Assessments and Interventions for ADD Students.* Irvine,
CA, KC Publishing, 1992.

terfere with completing classwork (school column) or homework or chores (home column)? It is advisable to explore
the last column with the patient alone, because persons with
ADHD often have a front of bravado about the effect on
their mood and self-esteem. A diagnosis requires some problems of pathologic extent in at least two columns.

Structured diagnostic interviews offer another option.
Though most were developed for research purposes, some

	Not at All	Just a Little	Quite a Bit	Very Much

are in computer-assisted versions suitable for administration by an office assistant after appropriate training. For example, the Diagnostic Interview Schedule for Children (DISC 4) checks each of the DSM-IV symptoms of ADHD with four questions each, and similarly reviews DSM-IV symptoms of common comorbid disorders. It takes 1 to 1.5 hours, depending on how much pathology is discovered. A structured interview especially developed for clini-

	At Home: Homework, Chores, Family Relations	School or Work: Lessons, Jobs, Tasks, Peer Relations
Global function		
Attention, focus, completion		
Activity level, organization		
Impulse control		
Comorbidities		

Figure 2-2: ADHD History Worksheet

Adapted with permission of C. Keith Conners, PhD, 1998.

cal use by trained lay assistants is the Children's Interview for Psychiatric Syndromes (ChIPS).[5] Most structured interviews are available in regular versions (administered directly to patients more than 11 years old) and in parent versions. All results of lay-administered structured interviews must be reviewed by a clinician, making use

Community, Social, Clubs, Sports, Scouts, 4-H, Peers	Mood, Self-Esteem, Self-Image, Aspirations/Hopes

of all available information, and clinical judgment should override the computerized decision if there is a discrepancy. No clinical diagnosis (or exclusion thereof) should be based solely on a structured interview or rating scale alone, but these instruments can save clinicians' time by systematically gathering information for clinician review.

Table 2-1: Diagnostic Pitfalls

Depending solely on any of the following for diagnosing ADHD is risky:

Pitfall	Reason for Inadequacy
Relying on a diagnostic trial of stimulant	Not pathognomonic; stimulants improve attention and improve impulse control regardless of diagnosis or normality, and fail to help a few patients who really have ADHD.
Depending on observation in office	Inadequate time sample: must be based on *history* of consistent or repeated pattern, but symptoms do not usually appear in all settings, especially novel ones, and are often suppressed in a one-to-one, especially with unfamiliar adult.
Accepting a global statement of family or teacher that the patient is 'hyperactive' or 'has ADHD'	Hyperactivity, ADHD, or just 'hyper' have become popular catch-all terms used indiscriminately for many problems. The specific symptoms must be characterized, and the reliability of informants must be considered.

A site license for the computer-assisted DISC 4 can be obtained by calling Columbia DISC at 212-543-5948 or e-mailing disc@worldnet.att.net; price is negotiable according to intended use. A ChIPS paper-and-pencil kit (including manual) can be obtained for about $115 from American Psychiatric Press, Inc., 1400 K St., NW., Washington, DC 20005; phone 800-368-7777, fax 202-789-2648,

Pitfall	Reason for Inadequacy
Relying exclusively on rating scales	Although rating scales are useful ways to quantify informants' impressions, diagnosis also depends on assessing impairment, duration, and pervasiveness, as well as on ruling out mimicking disorders.
Depending on tests	There is no pathognomonic test for ADHD. Although neuro-psychologic tests, MRIs and EEGs document group differences between ADHD and normal controls, such tests are not useful for diagnosing individuals. Psychometric tests have some use, but are often not necessary. Diagnosis is made *by history*, not by tests.

www.appi.org. A computer-assisted version should be available by the time this book is published.

How Not to Make the Diagnosis

A clinician should not depend on the popular or intuitive tactics in Table 2-1 to make a decision about diagnosis. An ADHD diagnosis should be considered only with extreme caution below age 3 because of possible confusion with the normal developmental high activity level of toddlers. In particular, a preverbal child may improve attention span and calm down remarkably on attaining fluent speech.

How to Rule Out Mimicking Disorders

An elementary mimicking disorder to rule out is epilepsy, either petit mal or atypical partial seizures. The distinction from ADHD is usually readily apparent from the episodic nature of the seizures, characterized by staring and unresponsiveness. In addition to attention lapses, complex partial seizures can sometimes involve frenzied activity that a family member or teacher might call hyperactivity. Again, the episodic nature of such activity makes the distinction from ADHD. Seizure disorder is a special example of the fallacy of a diagnostic trial of a stimulant; amphetamine is slightly anticonvulsant and a seizure disorder might respond, even though a stimulant is not the treatment of choice. An electroencephalogram, of course, is indicated whenever a seizure disorder is suspected.

The main tools for ruling out other mental disorders that can mimic ADHD are additional history and mental status examination, including observation and interview of the patient alone, as well as with parents or significant others. Table 2-2 lists common features of other mental disorders that overlap with ADHD. Features that distinguish them from ADHD are listed in the last row. Substance abuse can mimic any mental disorder. In addition, both ADHD and learning disorder (LD) can result in academic underperformance, either separately or together, and sometimes need individual psychoeducational testing to make the distinction. ADHD alone can cause low grades, failure, and underachievement on group testing (in which distractibility and attention span take a toll on the test score) but not on individual testing with optimized conditions. If routine group achievement tests are up to ability/age level, LD can be ruled out without individual testing;

if not, individual testing is needed. Receptive language disorder can mimic some inattention symptoms (eg, not seeming to listen, not following instructions).

If the patient meets criteria for another mental disorder (including learning or language disorder) that explains all of the symptoms, this should become the working diagnosis rather than ADHD. However, such disorders not only can mimic ADHD, but also at times can mask underlying ADHD. If the working-diagnosis disorder is treated and the ADHD symptoms persist, both diagnoses may be in order, and both can be addressed in the treatment plan. In fact, comorbidity is common in ADHD.

Comorbidity

The diagnostic challenge is compounded by the high rate of comorbidity in ADHD. The AAP guidelines emphasize the importance of searching for coexisting conditions.[2] ADHD is usually present lifelong, with the other disorder(s) accruing later, except for language and learning disorder, which also manifest early. All of the disorders listed in Table 2-2 except autism can develop in the presence of ADHD and, in fact, seem more likely than in the random population. For example, 25% or more of patients with ADHD also have a diagnosable anxiety disorder[6,7] (not counting simple phobias). A significant proportion have mood disorders, and sometimes depression from the discouragement resulting from ADHD. Mood disorders are especially likely in adolescents and adults with ADHD. A higher-than-chance proportion of adults with schizophrenia have a history of ADHD.

However, the most common comorbidity (about half of most clinical ADHD samples) is the spectrum of antisocial behavior. The younger and milder form, called *oppositional-defiant disorder* (ODD), features negativism, hostility, provocativeness, disobedience, frequent tantrums, quick temper, argumentativeness, spitefulness, and a 'bad attitude.' Its more virulent form, *conduct disorder*,

Table 2-2: Mental Disorders That Can Mimic ADHD: Overlapping or Similar Signs and Symptoms

ADHD Symptoms	Depression	Bipolar (Manic)
Inattentiveness, distractibility, forgetfulness, losing things, careless mistakes	Impairment of concentration and memory; preoccupation with mood	Flight of ideas, thought racing, distraction by delusions of grandiosity
Failure to finish tasks or activities; reluctance to start if needs sustained mental effort	Fatigue, anergia, loss of interest	Flight of ideas/ activities; grandiosely above common tasks
Difficulty organizing	Anergia, cognitive impairment	Flightiness
Hyperactivity, fidgeting/squirming, restlessness, always on the go	Agitation	Hyperactivity, driven quality
Excessive talking	Agitated complaining	Pressured speech
Impulsive blurting of answers, interrupting, intruding		Pressured speech, flight of ideas, impulsive and poor judgment

Anxiety, Including PTSD and OCD	Psychosis	Autism
Preoccupation with worry or obsession; intrusive memories/ flashbacks, psychic numbing, hypervigilance	Withdrawal from reality, preoccupation, loose association, 'distraction' by hallucinations	Disregard of people, unresponsiveness to attempted communication
Fear-induced paralysis of function; afraid to try, expecting failure; avoiding of reminders; perfectionism; not finishing	As above	Abrupt change of activity, resistance to instructed activity
	Psychotic fragmentation	
Panic, agitation, anxiety-driven restlessness, nervousness	Psychotic agitation, response to hallucinations	Hyperactivity, twirling, pacing, flapping
Anxious verbosity, obsessions, verbal rituals	Talking to hallucinations	Compulsive stereotyped repetitions
Anxious eagerness; reenactments; intrusive rituals	Responding to hallucination	Obliviousness of personal space of others

(continued on next page)

Table 2-2: Mental Disorders That Can Mimic ADHD: Overlapping or Similar Signs and Symptoms (continued)

ADHD Symptoms	Depression	Bipolar (Manic)
Impatience, easy frustration, difficulty waiting	Easy frustration	Pressured hyperactivity and impulsiveness
Irritability	Irritability	Irritability
Restless sleep	Insomnia	Insomnia
Lability, instability (emotional and physiologic)		Labile affect
Distinguishing from ADHD: (onset < age 7, chronic pattern)	Depressed mood, anorexia, weight loss, suicidal ideation, guilt feelings, psychomotor slowing, mutism, fatigue, episodic manifestation	Family history of mood disorder; extreme driven quality; sometimes episodic prominent mood: irritable, grandiose; possible appetite change, weight change; episodic onset at any age

Anxiety, Including PTSD and OCD	Psychosis	Autism
Intolerance of delay that builds suspense or reminds of trauma	Lack of social orientation, easy frustration	Lack of social orientation, easy frustration
Anger when rituals frustrated	Paranoid irritability	Irritability when rituals, routine interrupted
Insomnia or nightmares	Nocturnal agitation, insomnia	Nocturnal agitation, insomnia
Physiologic instability, nervousness	Psychotic unpredictability	Lability, unpredictability
Phobias, worries, stress-induced onset, obsession, compulsions, perfectionism, tremor, physiologic symptoms (palpitations, shortness of breath, sweating), posttraumatic play; onset at any age	Delusions, poverty of thought, disorientation, command hallucinations, inappropriate affect	Impaired non-verbal/verbal communication, lack of social relatedness, fantasy, or social or imaginative play

often develops from earlier ODD and is marked by bullying, running away, conning, breaking in, fighting with weapons, cruelty, setting fires, theft, extortion, robbery, sexual imposition, truancy, vandalism, and assault. In some cases, the adult outcome is antisocial personality disorder. ODD behavior is often manifested toward the parent in the presence of the clinician (sometimes even to the clinician), while the signs and symptoms of conduct disorder are often exposed only by historical probing, especially of the child alone, who may report delinquency unknown to (or hidden from or ignored by) the parent. Diagnosis of this comorbidity requires a persistent pattern of antisocial behavior not attributed to subcultural norms and the conduct disorder must be manifested in at least three types of delinquent activity. A single incident or conformity to a deviant subculture does not qualify for diagnosis.

A statistically rare but clinically devastating comorbidity is Tourette's disorder, marked by chronic multiple motor and phonic tics (involuntary contractures of muscle groups). The most severe cases may involve coprolalia (barking of obscene words), flailing/ballistic tics that dislocate joints, or self-hitting tics that can lead to severe injuries, including retinal detachment. Even cases without extreme symptoms can interfere with daily activities such as writing, speaking, reading, or eating. About 1% to 2% of ADHD cases have or will develop Tourette's or its partial expressions (chronic motor tic or chronic vocal tic), a risk that is an order of magnitude higher than in the random population (0.05% for Tourette's). Half or more of Tourette's patients also have ADHD (a mathematical quirk of the vast difference in prevalence of the two disorders). When they occur together, ADHD usually precedes Tourette's by 2 to 4 years. Therefore, children with ADHD should be monitored for development of tics as part of the extended evaluation.

However, Tourette's (and related multiple chronic motor tics or multiple chronic vocal tics) must be distinguished from the much more common and benign transient tic (less than a year duration and often only a single tic). The latter affects up to 20% of school-age boys and is often not impairing; sometimes neither child nor parent may notice the tic until it is called to their attention by a clinician. It should only be diagnosed as a disorder if it is distressing or impairing in some way. Further, tic disorder must be distinguished from tics as a side effect of stimulant medication, which resolve when the dose is lowered or discontinued. Any impairing tic disorder, especially suspicion of Tourette's, warrants referral to a clinician experienced in its evaluation and treatment, at least for initial consultation.

Developmental coordination disorder is a common comorbidity that has been de-emphasized since the designation 'minimal brain dysfunction' was abandoned. Nevertheless, it can be a significant problem for some patients, complicating the inattention to detail, interfering with performance in sports and crafts, and aggravating the accident proneness. It may cause sloppy penmanship and slow completion of written work. It is manifested in such things as impaired visual-motor coordination, impaired fine and gross motor coordination, and neurologic 'soft signs.' It should not be diagnosed unless it impairs academic performance or activities of daily living.

Mental retardation and ADHD co-occur at a rate higher than chance, but the vast majority of patients with ADHD have normal intelligence, some even superior. When diagnosing ADHD in the presence of mental retardation, it is important to compare the attentional ability, impulse control, and activity level to the *mental* age, not chronological age.

Maltreatment is not a comorbidity but needs to be mentioned because, in some samples of abused children, 20%

Table 2-3: Etiologic Evaluation of ADHD (treatable causes only)

Possible Cause of ADHD[9]	Focus of History
Thyroid abnormality (2% to 5% of ADHD)	Heat or cold intolerance, excess weight gain/loss
Food sensitivity or allergy (food or additive) (probably 5% to 15% of ADHD but not established [higher in preschoolers])	Diet history, deviant food preferences, infant formula intolerance, other food intolerance, general allergies, eczema, asthma, behavioral improvement with antihistamine, itches, sleep disturbance, somatic complaints, frequent antibiotics, hypoglycemic episodes, timing re: meals
Lead or other heavy metal poisoning or other toxin (insecticide, solvent, etc) (prevalence variable by region, neighborhood, probably a low proportion on average)	Ingestion/play habits, environment, remodeling ('gentrification'), industrial proximity, agricultural or occupational exposure (parent's work clothes), onset of symptoms (timing)

have ADHD, 2 to 5 times the prevalence in the general population. Therefore, an abused child should be evaluated (at least cursorily) for ADHD, and vice versa. Another statistical association is teenage out-of-wedlock pregnancy, for which girls with ADHD are at higher risk than non-ADHD girls.[8]

Focus of Examination	Laboratory Work, Tests
Hair caliber, deep tendon reflexes, eye examination, neck palpation	Thyroid function tests if indicated by history and physical
Allergic signs: shiners (dark, puffy eyelids), nasal congestion, drainage, or itch, or allergic salute (swipes at nose with back of hand), upturned/creased nose, skin signs (rash, discoloration, reactiveness), wheezing	Skin tests for allergy/sensitivity to foods or additives; if positive, would help confirm etiology and guide treatment, but food sensitivities have a reported high false-negative rate, with disagreement among allergists about existence, value, and meaning.
Poisoning stigmata (eg, lead line, skin color), general vigor, robustness	Tissue levels of suspected toxins if indicated by H and P. Test routinely in neighborhoods with high endemic rates of specific toxin(s).

(continued on next page)

Etiologic Evaluation

Diagnosing ADHD does not complete the diagnostic task. The cause must be searched. In most cases, the main cause is a genetic diathesis or some other cause not directly treatable. Sometimes no definite cause can be determined. However, in a substantial minority of cases, a treatable cause can be

**Table 2-3: Etiologic Evaluation of ADHD
(treatable causes only)** (continued)

Possible Cause of ADHD[9]	Focus of History
Nutritional deficiency or relative deficiency: iron, zinc, magnesium, calcium, vitamins, protein, essential fatty acids, especially of n-3 series. (prevalence variable by SES and subculture)	Diet history, restrictive or deviant food preferences, dry skin, itch, thirst, fatigue, anergia, general health, growth rate, hypoglycemic episodes, symptom timing relative to meals, use of dietary supplements (eg, vitamin pills)
Autoimmune or other disorder of immunity (prevalence undetermined in ADHD, but association established, may vary by climate; probably small proportion of ADHD)	Streptococcal infection and sequelae (Sydenham's, rheumatic fever, tics, obsessive-compulsive disorder), frequent need for antibiotics, thyroiditis, vaccine reaction, other immune or autoimmune dysfunction
Chronic medication side effects or toxicity (low proportion)	Anticonvulsants; anti-asthmatics (β-agonists, corticoids); chronic antibiotics; decongestants; OTC use; herbals

found. The medical history and physical examination should focus on the areas demonstrated to be causally linked to small subgroups of ADHD. As suggested by Table 2-3, key areas for clarification include diet, environmental and medical

Focus of Examination	Laboratory Work, Tests
General health, metabolic vigor, percentile on growth chart, pallor (nail beds, conjunctiva), GI symptoms, cardiovascular compensation, other physical findings, especially if not easily explained	Tissue levels of any mineral suspected borderline or deficient; general screening in puzzling cases; for suspected deficiency with imbalanced diet, diagnostic trial of RDA multivitamins (with or without minerals)
Neurologic dysfunctions: tics, chorea, athetosis, incoordination, excessive soft signs; heart murmur; signs of chronic low-grade infection (temp? tonsils? nodes? sinus?) collagen disease, allergy, other immune dysfunction	ASO titer, SED rate, CBC, throat or other culture if indicated by H and P; other tests as suggested by H and P
According to suspected drug	Blood level of drug if toxicity suspected; diagnostic switch of drug if feasible

exposure, and allergic diathesis. It should be noted that many of these causes have been overstated by various advocacy groups to the point where the claims have lost credibility. However, a scientific review for the November 1998 NIH

Consensus Development Conference on ADHD found evidence for the relevance to small subgroups of ADHD.[9] When relevant, they may be aggravating causes rather than sole causes. Note that Table 2-3 lists only treatable causes. Untreatable causes, such as genetics, fetal alcohol effects, and perinatal brain trauma, are important and may have implications for prevention, though not for treatment.

Evaluating Strengths of Patient and Parents or Significant Others

Part of the data for treatment planning is a summary of the patient's strengths and resources: intelligence, motivation, sense of humor, flexibility, social skills, interest in treatment, etc. One of the patient's resources should be support from parents or significant others. In this highly heritable disorder, one or both parents may have trouble organizing to carry out a treatment plan. The reliability and validity of a parent or significant other as informant are important not only for initial diagnosis, but also for monitoring treatment results.

References

1.   American Psychiatric Association. *Diagnostic and Statistical Manual of Mental Disorders*, 4th ed (DSM-IV). Washington, DC, American Psychiatric Association, 1994.

2.   Diagnosis and evaluation of the child with attention-deficit/hyperactivity disorder. American Academy of Pediatrics. *Pediatrics* 2001;105:1158-1170.

3.   Wolraich ML, Felice ME, Drotar D, eds. *The Classification of Child and Adolescent Mental Diagnoses in Primary Care: Diagnostic and Statistical Manual for Primary Care (DSM-PC)*. Elk Grove, IL, American Academy of Pediatrics, 1996.

4.   Wolraich ML, Feurer I, Hannah JN, et al: Obtaining systematic teacher report of disruptive behavior disorders utilizing DSM-IV. *J Abnorm Child Psychol* 1998;26:141-152.

5.   Teare M, Fristad MA, Weller EB, et al: Study I: development and criterion validity of the Children's Interview for Psychiatric Syndromes. *J Child Adolesc Psychopharmacol* 1998;8:205-211.

6. Biederman J, Faraone SV, Spencer T, et al: Patterns of psychiatric comorbidity, cognition, and psychosocial functioning in adults with attention-deficit/hyperactivity disorder. *Am J Psychiatry* 1993;150:1792-1798.

7. Pliszka SR: Comorbidity of attention-deficit/hyperactivity disorder: an overview. *J Clin Psychiatry* 1998;59:50-58.

8. Arnold LE: Sex differences in ADHD: conference summary. *J Abnorm Child Psychol* 1996;24:555-569.

9. Arnold LE: Treatment alternatives for ADHD. In: *Abstracts of NIH Consensus Development Conference on Diagnosis and Treatment of ADHD*. Bethesda, MD, NIH, 1998. Complete review in *J Attention Disord* 1999;3:30-48.

Chapter 3

Selecting Treatment for a Patient: Overview of Treatment Planning and Strategy

reatment planning for ADHD should be based on a thorough understanding of the patient's problems, strengths, and preferences. All problems must be addressed, including those that the patient or family present with (chief complaint) and those that the clinician notes in the process of evaluation (diagnosis, comorbidity, and causes; see Chapter 2). The clinician can best address these problems only when the chosen treatment strategy is acceptable to family members, is one with which they are capable of cooperating, and is supported by available resources, including patient strengths and support from family, teacher, coach, employer, etc. Table 3-1 lists these basic considerations.

Treat Causes When Possible

Treatments for ADHD can be classified several ways. The most popular method, and the one used for subsequent chapters, is according to stimulants, other drugs, behavioral therapy, and other (sometimes called alternative) treatments. A better classification for establishing an effective treatment strategy may be that depicted in Table 3-2. When a specific cause can be identified in an individual case, it should be addressed by appropriate treatment before resorting to generic treatments.[1] Generic treatments, such as stimulant medication, help most patients with ADHD so dramatically that the clinician may be tempted to implement them immediately without looking for specific causes. No matter how tempting, convenient, and effective this approach may be, it is not optimal medical care for some patients. For the few cases with a treatable cause, it would be analogous to treating streptococcal pharyngitis with aspirin, fluids, and salt-water gargling while overlooking an antibiotic. These are respectable, effective treatments for sore throat and temperature elevation, and may be the best that could be done for a viral sore throat, but are unduly focused on symptoms at the expense of noting and treating the cause.

Unfortunately, in the overwhelming majority of patients with ADHD, no treatable cause can be found, or the cause is not directly treatable given the current state of medical knowledge (eg, genetic, prenatal infection, head trauma). Also, in some cases that can be treated specifically, the response may not be complete and may need supplementation with a generic treatment. Therefore, the vast majority of patients with ADHD need one or more of the generic, symptom-targeted treatments.

Beware Vicious Circles

A treatment strategy must recognize and address any vicious circles that may have developed (Figure 3-1). Especially for older children, adolescents, and adults, deviation-amplifying feedback loops may result in considerable secondary pathology and contribute to maintaining symptoms. This phenomenon can mask treatment benefit to the extent of making an actually effective treatment appear ineffective by global assessment. For example, even if the original inattention, im-

Table 3-1: Basic Principles of Treatment (Tx) Planning

Strategy	Reason	How
Treat causes where possible.	Superior medical practice	Look for causes (see Chapter 2).
Build therapeutic alliance and structure to last over time.	Chronic disorder requires chronic treatment.	Ally with patient's strengths and resources (including supportive family, teacher).
Make sure treatment is acceptable (palatable) to patient and family.	Unpalatable treatments lead to noncompliance; without compliance, any treatment is ineffective.	Overview of Tx alternatives. Explain, check for feedback, answer questions, look for nonverbal signs of concern, hesitation, negative reaction.
Enlist patient's active participation, even if a young child.	For treatment of chronic disorder, patient must ultimately take responsibility.	Establish rapport, address child, ask child's opinion, ask child to help track treatment effect.

pulsiveness, and overactivity are ameliorated or eliminated by a stimulant, behavioral, academic, or work problems can continue, maintained by the psychosocial vicious circles shown. Methods for preventing and treating such complications are addressed in Chapters 6 and 8.

Strategy	Reason	How
Consider comorbidity, as well as urgency of ADHD symptoms.	Affects treatment choice; treatment should address comorbidity as well as ADD.	Rate severity/urgency; list comorbidity; get patient and family input.
Consider expense to family: financial, emotional, and temporal resources.	Resources will be needed for long haul in this chronic disorder; a treatment spurt followed by exhaustion and lapse is not useful.	Be aware of various Tx costs, including common drugs, and coverage for them. Consult with family about what can be sustained.
Select treatment with good leverage.	Efficiency and simplicity	See text and Table 3-3.
Capitalize on strengths of patient, family, social network.	Efficiency, good medical practice	Look for strengths. See text and Chapters 5, 6, and 8

American Academy of Pediatrics Clinical Practice Guideline for Treatment of the School-Aged Child with Attention-Deficit/Hyperactivity Disorder

The American Academy of Pediatrics (AAP) has published the *Clinical Practice Guideline for Treatment of*

Table 3-2: Types of Treatments for ADHD Classified by Specificity/ Generalizability and Target

All treatments listed have some (at least suggestive) literature evidence of efficacy, but not always conclusive. See later chapters for description and limitations of supporting evidence. Most of the cause-targeted treatments are considered 'alternative' in the most popular classification.[1]

Specific Cause-Targeted Treatments, Applicable to Small Subgroups

- Thyroid
- Detoxification (deleading, chelation)
- Desensitization or immune therapy
- Elimination (oligoantigenic or Few Foods) diets
- Nutrient supplementation for diagnosed deficiency states (Fe, Zn, Mg, Ca, vitamins)

Generic Symptom-Targeted Treatments, Useful for Most Patients

- Psychoactive medications
  - Stimulants
  - Antidepressants
  - α_2-agonists
  - Tranquilizers/neuroleptics and other medications

School-Aged Children with Attention-Deficit/Hyperactivity Disorder,[2] an excellent summary of some basic treatment principles for that age group. The guideline cautions that "...it is not intended as a sole source of guidance for the treatment of children with ADHD... and may not provide the only appropriate approach... the recommendations

- Behavioral treatments
  - Behavior modification
  - Parent training/guidance
  - Teacher consultation
  - Daily report card
  - Home token economy
  - Skill/organization training
  - EMG biofeedback with relaxation training
- Supportive treatment, counseling, groups, family therapy

Treatments With Insufficient Evidence for Classification

- EEG biofeedback
- Vestibular stimulation
- Channel-specific perceptual training
- Various other experimental treatments (herbals, essential fatty acids, acupuncture, etc)

in this statement do not indicate an exclusive course of treatment or serve as a standard of medical care."[2] Accordingly, this book, although highly compatible with the guideline, is not constrained by it. For example, the scope of the book is broader, and specific recommendations may vary slightly based on my understanding of the literature

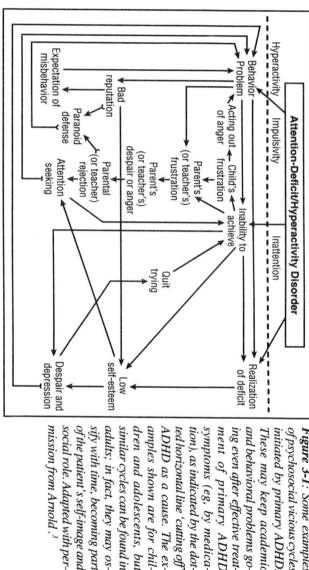

Figure 3-1: *Some examples of psychosocial vicious cycles initiated by primary ADHD. These may keep academic and behavioral problems going even after effective treatment of primary ADHD symptoms (eg, by medication), as indicated by the dotted horizontal line 'cutting off' ADHD as a cause. The examples shown are for children and adolescents, but similar cycles can be found in adults; in fact, they may ossify with time, becoming part of the patient's self-image and social role. Adapted with permission from Arnold.[3]*

and 33 years of clinical experience and research focused on ADHD.

The five main recommendations of the AAP Guideline are summarized in Table 3-3 for easy reference, and the recommended clinical algorithm applying them is reproduced in Figure 3-2. These are elaborated in various chapters throughout the book. The third recommendation (Table 3-3) should be qualified by the addition of the statement, "when no treatable specific cause can be identified or when such a cause has been treated and residual symptoms are impairing." The guideline, in fact, recognizes the limitations of stimulants and behavioral treatment and the desirability of "more lasting or even curative" treatments.[2]

Therefore, the comment box at Step 2 in the clinical algorithm in Figure 3-2 should be modified by inserting the words, "treatment of any identifiable cause." Thus, box 2 should have the following three points under step 3 (instead of the listed two): (A) primary care clinicians should establish a treatment program that recognizes ADHD as a chronic condition; (B) any treatable cause that can be identified should be treated first; and (C) if no treatable cause or if impairing symptoms remain after such treatment, the clinician recommends stimulant medications and/or behavior therapy to improve target outcomes.

Evidence-based Treatment and Relative Efficacy

As might be expected with a multiplicity of treatments, no one treatment is fully effective and safe for all patients with ADHD, and some treatments are better than others. Controlled studies allow for general statements about comparative effectiveness of treatments at the group level (eg, average relative effect). For comparison, average treatment effect is often stated in terms of effect size (Cohen's d, the difference in means between treated and control groups divided by the standard deviation—ie, the number of standard deviations by which the treatment makes a difference).

Table 3-3: Summary of American Academy of Pediatrics Clinical Practice Guideline Recommendations for Treatment of a School-Aged Child with ADHD

1. Primary care clinicians should establish a treatment program that recognizes ADHD as a chronic condition.* In support of this goal, clinicians should:
   - Provide information about the condition.
   - Update and monitor family knowledge and understanding on a periodic basis.
   - Counsel about family response to the condition.
   - Develop appropriate education for the child about ADHD, with updates as the child matures.
   - Be available to answer the family's questions.
   - Ensure coordination of health and other services.
   - Help families set specific goals in areas related to the child's condition and its effect on daily activities.
   - If possible, link families with other families with children who have similar chronic conditions.

2. The treating clinician, parents, and child, in collaboration with school personnel, should specify appropriate target outcomes to guide management.** Example target outcomes to be considered include:
   - Improvements in relationships with parents, siblings, teachers, and peers.
   - Decrease in disruptive behaviors.
   - Improved academic performance, particularly in volume of work, efficiency, completion, and accuracy.

2. *(continued)*
   - Increased independence in self-care and/or homework.
   - Improved self-esteem.
   - Enhanced safety in the community, such as in crossing streets or riding a bicycle.

3. The clinician should recommend stimulant medication and/or behavior therapy as appropriate to improve target outcomes.
   - For children taking stimulants, if one does not work at the highest feasible dose, the clinician should recommend another.

4. When the selected management plan has not met target outcomes, clinicians should:
   - Re-evaluate the original diagnosis.
   - Use all of the appropriate treatments.
   - Check adherence to the treatment plan.
   - Evaluate for the presence of coexisting conditions.

5. The clinician should periodically provide a systematic follow-up for the child with ADHD. Monitoring should be directed to target outcomes and adverse effects, with information gathered from parents, teachers, and the child.

* As with other chronic conditions, treatment of ADHD requires the development of child-specific treatment plans that describe the methods and goals of treatment and means of monitoring care over time, including specific plans for follow-up.

**Target outcomes should derive from the key symptoms and specific impairments of the particular child.

Used with the permission of the Academy of Pediatrics. From *Pediatrics* 2001;108:1033-1044.

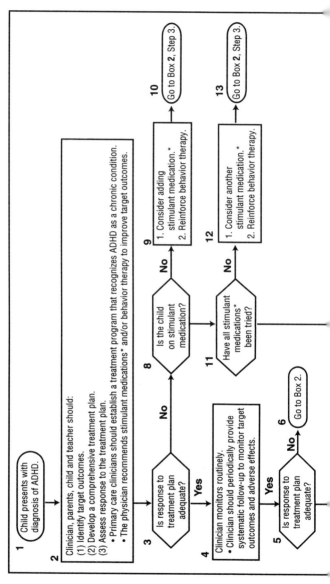

1 Child presents with diagnosis of ADHD.

2 Clinician, parents, child and teacher should:
(1) Identify target outcomes.
(2) Develop a comprehensive treatment plan.
(3) Assess response to the treatment plan.
 • Primary care clinicians should establish a treatment program that recognizes ADHD as a chronic condition.
 • The physician recommends stimulant medications* and/or behavior therapy to improve target outcomes.

3 Is response to treatment plan adequate?

Yes → **4** Clinician monitors routinely.
 • Clinician should periodically provide systematic follow-up to monitor target outcomes and adverse effects.

5 Is response to treatment plan adequate?

Yes → **6** Go to Box 2.

No (from 3) → **8** Is the child on stimulant medication?

No → **9**
1. Consider adding stimulant medication.*
2. Reinforce behavior therapy.

10 Go to Box 2, Step 3.

8 Yes → **11** Have all stimulant medications* been tried?

No → **12**
1. Consider another stimulant medication.*
2. Reinforce behavior therapy.

13 Go to Box 2, Step 3.

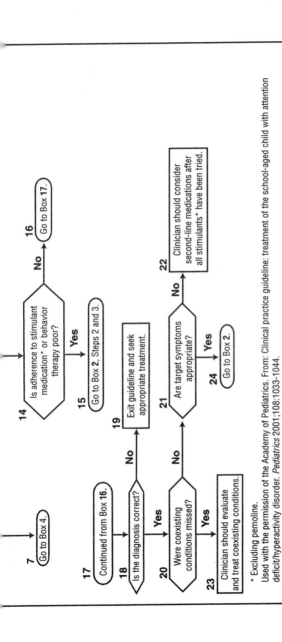

Figure 3-2: *Algorithm from the 2001 Clinical Guideline for the Treatment of School-Aged Children With ADHD published by the American Academy of Pediatrics.*

Text within the figure:

7 — Go to Box 4.

14 — Is adherence to stimulant medication* or behavior therapy poor?

No — 16 — Go to Box 17.

Yes — 15 — Go to Box 2, Steps 2 and 3.

17 — Continued from Box 16.

18 — Is the diagnosis correct?

No — 19 — Exit guideline and seek appropriate treatment.

Yes — 20 — Were coexisting conditions missed?

Yes — 23 — Clinician should evaluate and treat coexisting conditions.

No — 21 — Are target symptoms appropriate?

Yes — 24 — Go to Box 2.

No — 22 — Clinician should consider second-line medications after all stimulants* have been tried.

* Excluding pemoline.

Used with the permission of the Academy of Pediatrics. From: Clinical practice guideline: treatment of the school-aged child with attention deficit/hyperactivity disorder. *Pediatrics* 2001;108:1033–1044.

67

Table 3-4: Estimating Treatment Leverage and Matching the Treatment to the Patient

Certain patient characteristics have been reported as predicting a better or worse response to certain treatments. Not all of the drugs listed have FDA-approved indications for ADHD, but all are supported by published reports or common clinical practice.

Patient Characteristic or Context	Highly Effective or Better Treatments
Specific cause identified by medical history and physical exam, laboratory	Specific treatment (thyroid, chelation/detoxification, Few Foods or oligoantigenic diet, or repletion of deficiency)[1]
Inattentive-type ADHD	Stimulants in low doses, individually titrated Other medications, especially antidepressants Organizational skills training
Hyperactive-impulsive-type ADHD	Stimulants, often in higher doses (individually titrated) Behavioral treatment (behavior modification, daily report card, home token economy, parent training) Other medications, especially α_2-agonists
Combined-type ADHD	Combination treatments, including treatments for subtypes

Patient Characteristic or Context	Highly Effective or Better Treatments
Comorbid depression (with ADHD)	Antidepressants (tricyclics, bupropion, or MAO inhibitors) Combination of stimulant and cognitive-behavioral therapy Combination of stimulant and SSRI
Comorbid anxiety (with ADHD)	Behavioral therapy Tricyclic antidepressant Buspirone or α_2-agonist (or β-blocker) Combination of stimulant and SSRI or other antianxiety agent
Comorbid oppositional-defiant or conduct disorder, aggression	Combination of stimulants (often in higher doses, individually titrated) with behavioral therapy (behavior modification, daily report card, token economy, parent training)
Comorbid learning disorder (with ADHD)	Special educational services (eg, remedial tutoring) combined with low-dose stimulant (individually titrated)
Comorbid Tourette's (with ADHD)	α_2-agonists Antidepressants Neuroleptics Stimulants in combination with one of above
Comorbid coordination disorder	Stimulant Motor skill drill, sensorimotor integration, adaptive physical education

(continued on next page)

Table 3-4: Estimating Treatment Leverage and Matching the Treatment to the Patient (continued)

Patient Characteristic or Context	Highly Effective or Better Treatments
Combined comorbidity (anxiety and oppositional or conduct disorder)	Combination stimulant and behavioral treatment
Poverty, especially with single parent	Behavioral treatment and psychosocial support, especially combined with medication, social work consultation
Patient or family opposed to medication	Intense behavioral treatment Meditation, relaxation training with electromyographic biofeedback, massage, job change (see also Chapter 7)

In subsequent chapters, effect sizes are quoted when available. For example, comparison of stimulant with placebo commonly yields an effect size (ES) of 0.9 to 1.2, which is considered large. An ES of 0.5 is medium. A pretest-posttest ES, which includes placebo effect and statistical regression to the mean ('uncontrolled'), would run considerably larger than the placebo-controlled ES for the same treatment. For example, pretest-posttest effect sizes

Patient Characteristic or Context	Highly Effective or Better Treatments
Interested, motivated teacher or employer	Consultation with teacher or employer about structuring work environment, use of behavior modification in school, daily report card, etc
Blaming of patient based on ignorance of disorder	Education of all parties about ADHD
History of seizures	Amphetamine rather than methylphenidate
History of failed trial on one stimulant	Different stimulant
History of failed adequate trials on three different stimulants	Behavioral treatment Reevaluation for specific treatable cause Antidepressant (other than SSRI) α_2-Agonist Buspirone Neuroleptic Anticonvulsant

for stimulants can approach 2.0. Although ES provides a way of comparing treatments, placebo or sham controls are not equally feasible or effective for all treatments. Sampling can also influence the ES. Therefore, the most useful comparisons are those designed within the same study. Evidence-based treatments are those for which controlled studies show clinically and statistically significant effect sizes, usually medium or more.

Leveraging Treatment Efforts

Regardless of how group or general relative effectiveness is determined, the same relative effectiveness may not apply to an individual patient. Treatment A may work better for patient P while treatment B works better for patient Q. Thus, a given treatment may be more effective and efficient—have more leverage—with one patient than another. Conversely, for a given patient, different treatments may have different leverages (Figure 3-3). Furthermore, treatments may be combined for additional leverage. Efficiency and simplicity of treatment efforts are facilitated by selecting for a given patient the treatment(s) with the most leverage for that patient.

Determinants of Treatment Leverage

Characteristics of the patient (including idiopathic drug sensitivities) and his or her family and social context (neighborhood, social class, school, coach, employer, etc) determine not only which treatments are possible, but also which are most effective in a given case. The first priority, of course, is treatment of a specific cause if one is found.[1] For example, David et al[4,5] in a controlled trial found a nonsignificantly better behavioral response to chelation than to stimulant treatment (both significantly better than placebo) in children with ADHD and blood lead levels over 25 µg/dL. Most children with thyroid abnormality and ADHD respond behaviorally to thyroid treatment.[6] Table 3-4 summarizes some other determinants of leverage that can help in selecting the most efficient treatment strategy for a given patient.

Incorporating Patient and Family Strengths Into the Treatment Plan

Patients with ADHD often have many resources and strengths, either in themselves or in a support network, (family, teacher, employer), that can be marshaled in sup-

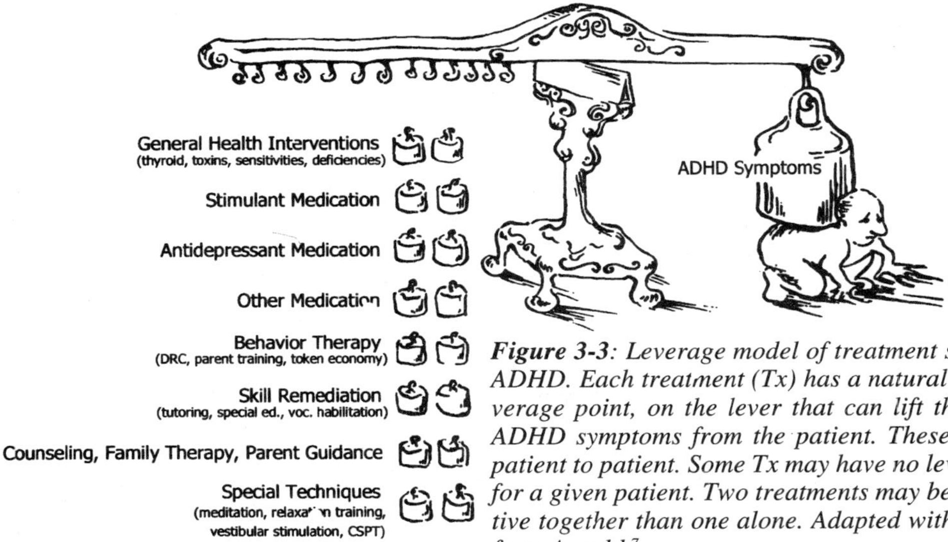

General Health Interventions
(thyroid, toxins, sensitivities, deficiencies)

Stimulant Medication

Antidepressant Medication

Other Medication

Behavior Therapy
(DRC, parent training, token economy)

Skill Remediation
(tutoring, special ed., voc. habilitation)

Counseling, Family Therapy, Parent Guidance

Special Techniques
(meditation, relaxa' 'n training, vestibular stimulation, CSPT)

ADHD Symptoms

Figure 3-3: Leverage model of treatment selection for ADHD. Each treatment (Tx) has a natural hook, or leverage point, on the lever that can lift the weight of ADHD symptoms from the patient. These differ from patient to patient. Some Tx may have no leverage at all for a given patient. Two treatments may be more effective together than one alone. Adapted with permission from Arnold.[7]

73

port of effective treatment and compensatory adjustment to the disorder. (Some of these were mentioned along with special problems in Table 3-4.) Many patients have intellectual strengths that, with some coaching, can be used for coping—eg, setting up a notebook or lists, breaking tasks into pieces that fit the attention span, rewarding oneself with a break after completing each task, eliminating distractions, counting to 10 before speaking, etc. Their high energy level may make them valued team members or hard workers, so a coach or employer may be willing to make some accommodations, such as frequent breaks or changes of task. Their spontaneity and creativity may allow them to think of coping tactics, especially with the aid of structured questioning. A brainstorming session with some families about treatment strategy might be productive. A parent who had to cope with the same problems and succeeded can be a good example as well as a good source of support. Chapters 5, 6, and 8 give more details about marshaling such strengths.

References

1.   Arnold LE: Treatment alternatives for ADHD. *Abstracts of NIH Consensus Development Conference on Diagnosis and Treatment of ADHD.* Bethesda, MD, NIH, 1998. Also in *J Attention Disord* 1999;3:30-48.

2.   Clinical practice guideline: treatment of the school-aged child with attention-deficit/hyperactivity disorder. *Pediatrics* 2001;108:1033-1044.

3.   Arnold LE: The art of medicating hyperkinetic children. *Clin Pediatr* 1973;12:35-41.

4.   David OJ, Hoffman SP, Sverd J, et al: Lead and hyperactivity. Behavioral response to chelation: a pilot study. *Am J Psychiatry* 1976;133:1155-1158.

5.   David OJ, Hoffman SP, Clark J, et al: The relationship of hyperactivity to moderately elevated lead levels. *Arch Environ Health* 1983;38:341-346.

6.   Weiss RE, Stein MA, Trommer B, et al: Attention-deficit hyperactivity disorder and thyroid function. *J Pediatr* 1993; 123:539-545.

7.   Arnold LE: Philosophy and strategy of medicating adults with minimal brain dysfunction. In: Bellak L, Grune, Stratton, eds. *Psychiatric Aspects of Minimal Brain Dysfunction in Adults*. The Psychological Corporation, 1979.

Chapter 4

Psychoactive Medications for ADHD: Drugs, Doses, and Effects

P sychoactive medicines, especially the sympathomimetic stimulants, are the best-documented and most rapidly effective treatments for most patients with ADHD, a fact recognized by the 1998 National Institutes of Health Consensus Development Conference.[1,2] Behavioral treatments also have well-documented effectiveness for most patients with ADHD,[1] but generally require intense, labor-expensive, multicomponent application to match the effectiveness achieved by stimulant medication. Even with intense behavioral protocols, supplementary medication is sometimes needed for severe cases.[2-4] Because such intense levels of behavioral treatment are not generally available, most patients with moderately to severely impairing ADHD symptoms who do not have a specifically treatable cause should consider a trial of psychoactive medication.

Priority Among Psychoactive Drugs

Table 4-1 lists the drugs that have been reported (not necessarily proven) useful in ADHD in the *approximate* order of documented effectiveness and desirability. This relative general priority and desirability of drug classes may be altered by individual patient features reviewed in previous chapters (Table 3-4). Within a class, several drugs may be equally effective statistically at the group level, but still differ in their idiosyncratic effects on individual patients.

It is important to note the well-documented superiority of stimulants for most children and adolescents,[5-7] a point made by the American Academy of Pediatrics Guideline.[8] Nevertheless, some individual patients, especially with certain comorbidities, may respond better to a different class. In adults, some antidepressants may equal stimulants,[9-11] although antidepressants tend not to be as effective for attention, and most have worse side effects. Stimulants are not only more efficacious in responders (about 90% of patients with ADHD[12,13]) but also safer than most other drugs. An exception is pemoline (Cylert®), which can cause liver necrosis in rare cases and can result in death or need for liver transplant. The safety of stimulants is important to note because they have received negative and even sensational press coverage, sometimes citing their DEA schedule II classification. Some clinicians are tempted to substitute a drug with a less favorable benefit-risk ratio, such as an antidepressant, α_2-agonist, or even neuroleptic, which may actually be more dangerous medically.

Relative Advantages and Side Effects

The different classes of drugs vary not only in general effectiveness and side effects, but also in their suitability for addressing comorbidity and other specific symptoms or dysfunction (Table 4-2). Because stimulants are so preeminent, the relative advantages of the two best-documented stimulants, methylphenidate (Concerta™, Metadate™, Methylin™, Ritalin®, Focalin™) and amphetamine (Adderall®, Dexedrine®), should be compared (Table 4-3), which can offer some guidance for first-line therapy.

However, the most important point about stimulants (and about drugs in any class) is that if the first one fails,

Table 4-1: Drugs Used For ADHD

Not all of these have been documented as effective by well-controlled studies, let alone carry FDA-approved indications for ADHD.

Generic Name	Brand Name	Usual Daily Dose[c] mg (mg/kg)
Stimulants (ES 0.8-2.0)		
amphetamine, racemic (dextro-levo)[a]	Benzedrine® (withdrawn)	10-40 (0.3-1)
dextroamphetamine[a,b]	Dexedrine®, Dextrostat®	5-30 (0.2-0.7)
levoamphetamine[a]	Cydril® (withdrawn)	14-42 (0.3-1)
mixture 3/4 d-, 1/4 l-amphetamine[a,b]	Adderall®	10-40 (0.3-1)
methamphetamine[b,d]	Desoxyn®	5-25 (0.2-0.7)
methylphenidate, racemic threo[a,b]	Ritalin®, Methylin™ Metadate™	10-60 (0.3-1.5)
osmotic release[a,b] (OROS®)	Concerta™▲	18-54 (0.3-1.5)
dextro-threo-methylphenidate[a]	Focalin™ *[b]	5-30 (0.2-0.7)
pemoline[a,b]	Cylert®	37.5-112.5 (1-3)

[a] Supported by controlled studies
[b] FDA-approved indication for ADHD
▲ Concerta™ is slow-release methylphenidate using the OROS® osmotic technology.
* Focalin™ is pure dextro-(threo) methylphenidate.

Generic Name	Brand Name	Usual Daily Dose[c] mg (mg/kg)
Antidepressants (ES 0.5-1.5)[e]		
imipramine (TCA)[a]	Tofranil®	20-100 (0.7-3)
desipramine (TCA)[a]	Norpramin®, Pertofrane®	20-100 (0.7-3)
amitriptyline (TCA)[a]	Elavil®, Endep®	20-100 (0.7-3)
nortriptyline (TCA)	Pamelor®	10-50 (0.4-2)
bupropion[a] [14]	Wellbutrin®	75-300 (3-6)
clomipramine (TCA)[a]	Anafranil®	25-100
tranylcypromine (MAOI A+B)[a]	Parnate®	5-15
clorgyline (MAOI A)[a]		5-20
pargyline (MAOI)	Eutonyl®	
venlafaxine[f]	Effexor®	25-100 (1.4)
SSRIs (eg, fluoxetine[f])	Prozac®	5-40

[c] Usual daily dose should not be interpreted as either a cap or a minimal effective dose if a higher or lower dose is clinically indicated in individual cases. See Table 4-6. Actual patient doses must be individually titrated, using direct teacher and parent information.

[d] Although it carries an FDA-approved indication for ADHD, methamphetamine, in contrast to other forms of amphetamine, is not favored by many experts because of suspected neurotoxicity in animal data.

(continued on next page)

Table 4-1: Drugs Used For ADHD (continued)

Generic Name	Brand Name	Usual Daily Dose[c] mg (mg/kg)
α₂-Agonists **(ES 0.3-5.0, depending on patient selection)**		
guanfacine[a]	Tenex®	0.5-4.0 (0.02-0.06)
clonidine (also patch)[a 15]	Catapres®	0.05-0.3 (0.002-0.005)
Miscellaneous (ES variable)		
buspirone (ES<1)	BuSpar®	5-30 (0.2-0.6)
diphenhydramine	Benadryl®	75-150
nicotine (adults only, ES>1)[a]	(lower dose for nonsmokers)	7-21 mg patch
modafinil	Provigil®	50-400
atomoxetine[g] (ES=1)[a]	not on market	dose not est. probably (0.05-1.5)
Anticonvulsants (ES up to 1.0)		
carbamazepine[a 16]	Tegretol®	50-800, serum level
valproate	Depakote®, Depakene®	serum level
phenytoin	Dilantin®	50-300

[e] No antidepressants are FDA-approved for ADHD, despite well-controlled studies demonstrating efficacy for many of them. In fact, some (but not all) studies show imipramine, desipramine, amitriptyline, and tranylcypromine equal to stimulants, though with worse side effects. For adults, they may equal stimulants despite not seeming to benefit attention as much as behavior.

·

Generic Name	Brand Name	Usual Daily Dose[c] mg (mg/kg)
Neuroleptics (ES usually about half of stimulants)[h]		
thioridazine[a]	Mellaril®	25-150 (1-6)
haloperidol[a,b]	Haldol®	0.5-5.0 (0.03-0.075)
chlorpromazine[a,b]	Thorazine®	25-150 (1-6)
risperidone	Risperdal®	0.25-2.0 (0.01-0.1)

[f] Despite a report of a positive open trial of fluoxetine, most experts do not consider selective serotonin reuptake inhibitors (SSRIs) generally effective for ADHD core symptoms, in contrast with the documented effectiveness of other antidepressant classes. The newer antidepressants, with both serotonin and catecholamine action (such as venlafaxine and nefazodone) are expected to be effective.

[g] Atomoxetine, a selective norepinephrine reuptake inhibitor, has shown significant effect on ADHD symptoms in premarketing controlled trials, with effect size of about 1.0,[17] but appropriate doses have not been established.

[h] Although haloperidol and chlorpromazine have FDA-approved indications for ADHD, neuroleptics should generally be a last resort because of the risk of tardive dyskinesia. The newer ones, such as risperidone, may carry less such risk.

[i] The precursors of neurotransmitters are nutrients found in the normal diet. They are included because they are used like drugs in supplemental dosage. Deanol (dimethylaminoethanol [DMAE]) was formerly marketed as Deaner®, but initial FDA approval was withdrawn; it was judged 'possibly effective.'

(continued on next page)

Table 4-1: Drugs Used For ADHD (continued)

Generic Name	Brand Name	Usual Daily Dose[c] mg (mg/kg)
Precursors (ES <0.6, short term)		
deanol (possible precursor of acetylcholine)[i]	Deaner®	500
tryptophan (precursor of serotonin)		(70-100)
tyrosine (precursor of dopamine and norepinephrine)		(100-140)
phenylalanine (precursor of dopamine and norepinephrine)		(100-140)
levo-DOPA (precursor of dopamine and norepinephrine)		
Others		
β-blockers, (eg, propranolol)	Inderal®	10-300
caffeine		100-450

Not ordinarily used: most minor tranquilizers, benzodiazepines

Contraindicated: barbiturates (aggravate hyperactivity; can even cause it)

ES = effect size, the number of standard deviations different from placebo or from pre-drug measure. It is a measure of clinical significance. An ES of 1 is considered large, 0.5 medium.

Adapted with permission from Arnold LE, Jensen PS: Attention-deficit hyperactivity disorder. In: Kaplan H, Sadock B, eds. *Comprehensive Textbook of Psychiatry.* Baltimore, Williams and Wilkins, 1995, pp 2295-2311.

the patient still has a good chance of responding to another in the same class. About two thirds of patients respond satisfactorily to either methylphenidate or amphetamine (compared to placebo); of the one third who do not respond, two thirds will respond to the other stimulant.[18] Furthermore, a patient poorly responsive to one isomer of a stimulant may respond to the other isomer of the same stimulant or to a mixture of the two isomers, or vice versa (see *Chiral Pharmacology* below). Ultimately, the only way to determine if a patient will respond to a given drug is to try it and carefully monitor the effect.

Chiral Pharmacology

Many psychoactive drugs, including stimulants, have stereoisomers (right- and left-hand shaped molecules, called dextro- and levo-). The dextroisomer of amphetamine has been well known as Dexedrine® and Dextrostat®. It and its mirror image, levoamphetamine, both have documented effectiveness compared to placebo,[19] but with some subtle differences (Table 4-4), including differential response in individual patients.[19,20] The racemic (dextro-levo) mixture (eg, Benzedrine®, withdrawn from the market) has also been reported to be effective in some patients who responded poorly to dextroamphetamine, and vice versa. Adderall® is a mixture of 75% dextroamphetamine and 25% levoamphetamine, and appears anecdotally to help some dextroamphetamine nonresponders (though not documented by controlled studies). Commercially available methylphenidate (eg, Concerta™, Metadate™, Methylin™, Ritalin®) has been racemic threo-methylphenidate—ie, dextro-levo-threo-methylphenidate. The dextro- isomer of methylphenidate (dextro-threo-methylphenidate, or d-methylphenidate for short) is being prepared for market under the trade name, Focalin™, undoubtedly with a subtly different response profile than racemic threo-methylphenidate. Preliminary reports suggest some advantages over racemic methylphenidate for

Table 4-2: Relative Advantages and Disadvantages/Side Effects of ADHD Drug Classes

Drug Class	Advantages
Stimulants	Specifically treat ADHD core symptoms of inattention, overactivity, and impulsiveness. Largest effect on ADHD of any drug class, especially for children. Significant benefit in 90% of ADHD if two or more tried in succession and titrated carefully. Calms comorbid aggression and oppositional-defiant behavior. Except for pemoline, medically safer than most psychoactive drugs. Results of given dose seen immediately; relatively easy titration.
Antidepressants tricyclics, bupropion, MAOIs,[21] probably newer antidepressants with both serotonin action and dopamine	Treat both ADHD and comorbid depression and anxiety. Helps some stimulant non-responders. Second most effective drug class for ADHD (except for SSRIs, which are not very effective). Some patients/families who are prejudiced against stimulants will accept antidepressants. May equal stimulant effectiveness for adults.

Side Effects, Disadvantages

Appetite loss
Sleep disturbance (if taken late)
Cramps (first few weeks)
Headaches
Mild BP and pulse increase
Evening crash
'Zombie' appearance (amphetamine look): constricted
  affect and spontaneity, emotional blunting
Depression
Tics
Hallucinations (skin crawling, visions)
Possible growth slowing first 2 years[22]
Dose for behavior may not be optimal for attention
Nuisance of schedule II Rx

Sedation
BP changes (down or up)
Dizziness (especially on standing)
Dry mouth
Cardiac conduction block; TCAs require
  ECG monitoring in children
Constipation, urinary retention (rare in children)
Headache (deserves evaluation)
Overdose lethal, and sudden deaths at
  therapeutic dose (DMI).
Response delayed, especially bupropion
Dietary restrictions for MAOIs
Not as good as stimulants for attention

(continued on next page)

Table 4-2: Relative Advantages and Disadvantages/Side Effects of ADHD Drug Classes (continued)

Drug Class	Advantages
α_2-Agonists	Treat both hyperactivity-impulsiveness and comorbid tic disorder or comorbid aggression. Helps some nonresponders to stimulants and antidepressants. Good for those overaroused, possibly with comorbid anxiety.
Buspirone	Good for comorbid anxiety and aggression, possibly depression. Relatively safe (similar to stimulants). Smooth effect. Relatively free of side effects.
Antihistamines (older)	Safe, cheap, over-the-counter. Especially good in patients with possible allergic etiology (but not restricted to those).
Neuroleptics	May work when stimulant does not, especially if stimulant makes worse. Good for comorbid anxiety, aggression, tic disorder, or bipolar disorder.
Anti-convulsants	Good for comorbid mood disorder, aggression, explosiveness, impulsiveness. May work when stimulant or anti-depressant does not.

TCA = tricyclic antidepressant
MAOI = monoamine oxidase inhibitor

Side Effects, Disadvantages

Response delayed
Sedation
Hypotensive dizziness (especially postural)
Dry mouth
Hypertensive rebound if dose missed
Sudden deaths (when used with stimulant)
Not as helpful for attention as stimulants

Possible paradoxic excitation
Several weeks needed to see full effect of a given dose,
  therefore hard/slow to titrate

Sedation
Risk of seizures in high doses
Not as effective as stimulants or antidepressants;
  unsatisfactory in many patients

Sedation
Extrapyramidal side effects
Endocrine effects
Tardive dyskinesia
Paradoxical agitation (akathisia)
Weight gain
Not specific, generally less effective than stimulants
Riskiest drug, last resort

Blood tests for levels and safety monitoring
Liver toxicity
Blood dyscrasia
Sedation or agitation
Ataxia

DMI = desipramine
SSRIs = selective serotonin reuptake inhibitors

Table 4-3: Relative Advantages of Methylphenidate (MPH) and Amphetamine (AMP) for Treatment of ADHD

Few of these are statistically significant; most are tendencies noted in more than one report in literature review.

Advantages of MPH	Advantages of AMP
Better continuous performance test response[a]	More consistent response day-to-day[a]
Better with comorbid Tourette's[a]	Higher proportion of patients with good/excellent response.[b,c] [23]
Better with visuomotor disorder[d]	Better with comorbid CD/ODD[d]
Possibly better with comorbid learning disorder[d]	Possibly better with high IQ[e]
Less anorexia[b]	Less depression/apathy[d]
Less weight loss[b]	Fewer stomach aches[d]

[a] Statistically significant in a controlled study

[b] Probable

[c] Of 174 patients in six placebo-controlled crossover studies, 48 responded better to amphetamine, 27 better to methylphenidate, and most of the rest to both.[24]

[d] Possible, suggested

[e] Significant in post hoc analysis of controlled study, but not replicated in prospective study

Advantages of MPH	Advantages of AMP
Less temporary growth suppression in low doses[d]	Safer with history of seizures[d]; slightly anticonvulsant in low doses[b]
Lower street value and abuse potential	Usually cheaper legally (generic)
Regular tablet strengths: 5, 10, 20 mg[f] SR strengths: 10, 20 mg	Adderall®: 5, 7.5, 10, 12.5, 15, 20, 30 mg tabs. Dexedrine® Spansule strengths: 5, 10, 15 mg Adderall® XR: 10, 20, 30 mg
A slow-release form using OROS® osmotic technology, Concerta™ 18, 36, and 54 mg, q.d., is now available	Slow-release Dexedrine® seems more consistently efficacious than slow-release Ritalin®
More readily available to Medicaid patients	Longer half-life

[f] Dextro-threo-methylphenidate Focalin™, when available, may be marketed in 2.5 mg as well as 5 and 10 mg. FDA approval pending.

Adapted with permission from Arnold LE: Methylphenidate vs amphetamine: a comparative review. *J Attention Disord* 2000;3(4):200-211.

Table 4-4: Differences and Relative Advantages of the Optical Stereoisomers of Amphetamine

	dextro- (Dexedrine®, Dextrostat®)	levo- (1/2 of Benzedrine®; 1/4 of Adderall®)
Dopaminergic vs norepinephrinergic	both actions equal	predominantly one, probably norepinephrinergic
Anorexia	more	little to none
'Amphetamine look' and 'zombie' appearance	more	less to none
Side effects in general	more	less
Visual-motor coordination[24]	improved	little or no effect
Aggression	controlled	equally controlled
Learning/ achievement	improved	much less improvement
Other symptoms	slightly better than levo- (statistically same in sample of 31)	not quite as good as dextro- (statistically same in sample of 31)

Adapted with permission from Arnold LE, Jensen PS: Attention-deficit hyperactivity disorder. In: Kaplan H, Sadock B, eds. *Comprehensive Textbook of Psychiatry*. Baltimore, Williams and Wilkins, 1995, pp 2295-2311.

some patients.[25] In many cases, the potencies of the chiral forms of the same drug differ, so, for example, the equipotent dose of the dextroisomer may be smaller in milligrams than for the levoisomer. Chiral pharmacology will undoubtedly become more important in the treatment of ADHD as we learn more about it. However, at this point, many of the subtle differences remain clinical impressions.

Sustained/Extended-Release Stimulant Preparations

The short half-life of most stimulants has evoked much clinical and research attention, with a search for longer-acting molecules and for better sustained-release preparations of methylphendidate and amphetamine. See Chapter 5 for details about the importance of preparations that avoid the need for school-time dosing. The available options have recently been expanded (Table 4-5). Not all extended-release forms are equal in duration, efficacy, or convenience. Except for the encapsulated beads, which could be poured out and swallowed individually or in creamy unchewed food if necessary, extended-release preparations must be swallowed whole to achieve the benefits of extended duration. This is not a trivial point, because a surprising proportion of young children chew their immediate-release tablets, and would do so with extended-release tablets if not instructed otherwise. The coated and uncoated tablets, even when swallowed whole, do not show consistent results. They seem to work well for some patients, but are disappointing in many cases. The encapsulated beads seem more consistently satisfactory. A unique delivery system, and perhaps the best so far, is the OROS® osmotic capsule-shaped tablet used in Concerta™. An external coating releases 22% of the medication immediately, and then an osmotic push compartment in the closed end of the three-compartment capsule acts like a slow piston and pushes two concentrations of drug out of

Table 4-5: Sustained/Extended-Release Options for Common Stimulants

Stimulant	Preparations
Methylphenidate	Concerta™*
	Metadate™ CD*
	Methylin™ ER
	Ritalin SR®
d-Amphetamine	Dexedrine® Spansule
3/4 d-Amphetamine, 1/4 l-Amphetamine	Adderall® XR

* Available only as extended-release.
▲ 18 mg Concerta™ delivers same blood level and clinical curves as 5 mg t.i.d. immediate release.

a laser-drilled hole in the other end over an 8+-hour period. This controlled release mimics the 12-hour blood levels and clinical response duration of t.i.d. immediate-release methylphenidate q 4 h, but with one morning dose.

Age and IQ Considerations

According to FDA-approved package inserts, virtually all of the drugs listed in Table 4-1 are not recommended for children below age 3, and most are not recommended below age 6. Some are not even recommended for older children. However, many of them, including all the stimulants, are commonly (perhaps too commonly) prescribed

Type/Form	Duration	Sizes
tablets with immediate-release overcoat and controlled osmotic delivery of remainder	12 h	18, 36, 54 mg▲
encapsulated beads with different dissolution times	8-9 h	20 mg
tablets	variable	10, 20 mg
coated tablets	variable	20 mg
encapsulated beads with different dissolution times	10-12 h	5, 10, 15 mg
encapsulated beads with different dissolution times	10-12 h	10, 20, 30 mg

for preschoolers, without glaring safety problems. Dextroamphetamine and Adderall® are approved for preschoolers down to age 3. Importantly, the limited data available suggest that stimulants are effective in preschoolers with ADHD, but at a lower rate than for older children.[26-28] In fact, it is not unusual for a child to show no benefit from a stimulant at age 5, but then show impressive benefit from a second trial of the same stimulant at age 7 or 8. This phenomenon may be related to brain or metabolic maturation and the normal transition around age 6 or 7 from preoperational thinking to concrete operational thinking.

This observation appears to apply more to mental age than to chronologic age, such that patients of any chronologic age with mental age below 4 or IQ below 45 seem less likely to respond favorably to a stimulant.[29] Certain developmental disorders that include hyperactivity as a component symptom, such as autism, often show idiosyncratic responses, either beneficial or deleterious.

Because of possible diagnostic confusion with the normal developmental high activity of toddlers, psychoactive drug treatment should be delayed if possible until after age 3 to observe development. Behavioral treatments can be implemented at any age, and should help prevent deterioration. A toddler with such severe hyperactivity that ADHD diagnosis and drug treatment are considered before age 3 should raise suspicion of a mood or other psychiatric disorder, and warrants evaluation by a child psychiatrist before treatment initiation (see Chapter 8).

At the opposite end of the age scale, a few controlled studies show that stimulant and antidepressant benefit for ADHD extend through adolescence into adulthood. Many experts suspect that the benefit of stimulants attenuates somewhat beyond puberty, although the benefit remains significant on group data.[30] Some studies suggest that, for adults, some antidepressants may be as effective as stimulants. For this reason and to prevent abuse, some experts tend to favor antidepressants for adults and even adolescents, at least for treatment initiated later in life. However, a good responder to stimulants should not be switched from a stimulant that is doing the job to an antidepressant just because of age. The ultimate decision about medication for any patient depends on that individual's own carefully monitored response to a specific drug.

First, Do No Harm

Any medication strong enough to help is also strong enough to harm. The medical axiom *primum non nocere* ('first, do not harm') applies as much to treatment of ADHD as to other disorders. This has two implications: (1) target impairment should be severe enough to warrant the risk; and (2) the clinician must be familiar with the risks and side effects of the various drugs, as well as their benefits (Table 4-2).

Sudden Deaths with Desipramine

The therapeutic safety margin for tricyclic antidepressants has always been considered narrow, with standard warnings about overdoses and precautions of electrocardiograms when the dose exceeds 3 mg/kg. The main problem is cardiac conduction slowing or blocking in multiple parameters. Several sudden deaths have been reported in patients taking desipramine (Norpramin®) at therapeutic doses for ADHD (without overdose). There is some controversy whether the reported number (a half dozen or fewer) significantly exceeds those expected by chance from imposing the prescription rate on the population base rate. Most experts suspect that this increase is significant, and do not make desipramine their first-choice drug for ADHD, given that other effective drugs are available. However, in some individuals, desipramine may work better than anything else, justifying the risk. Naturally, the electrocardiogram should be checked when prescribing dosages at the higher end of the therapeutic range. Some experts recommend a pretreatment electrocardiogram before prescribing any tricyclic antidepressant.

Sudden Deaths With Combination Clonidine and Stimulant

Experts disagree about the risks of combining clonidine (Catapres®) with a stimulant.[31-34] The main risk of clonidine by itself is rebound hypertension on sudden withdrawal. The popular practice of combining clonidine with a stimulant, theoretically cancelling side effects through their opposite actions, complicates the risk calculation. In particular, combining bedtime clonidine (to facilitate nocturnal settling and sleep) with daytime stimulant may risk aggravating daily physiologic mini-withdrawals of each of these short-half-life drugs. Alternating the two drugs may induce a daily cardiovascular pendulum swing. At least four sudden deaths have been reported in patients using the combination of clonidine and methylphenidate (not on clonidine alone); in all cases, patients had other complications, such as preexisting cardiac disease (two cases), recent general anesthesia, or other medications, so some experts discount all four cases. In patients with any known cardiac problem or taking other medications, the clinician should be cautious about this combination, especially if one drug is given as the other wears off in the daily dose regimen. Some experts routinely check the electrocardiogram before considering such a combination. A similar problem has not been reported for guanfacine (Tenex®), a drug of the same class with a longer half-life and presumably less withdrawal risk. But it has not been prescribed for ADHD as long as or as prevalently as clonidine, and is supported by only one controlled study.[35]

Pemoline Liver Necrosis

From the time pemoline (Cylert®) was first marketed, experts suspected an association with liver toxicity, and recommended monitoring of liver function tests. By 1996, enough evidence had accumulated to confirm the risk of rare irreversible liver necrosis, resulting in almost two dozen deaths or liver transplants over the 25-year experience. This demotes pemoline from a first-line drug to a second- or third-line choice. The rarity of the serious liver complications suggests that the risk is justified in specific patients with a good response who did not respond to a safer drug, and who have no history of liver problems. Liver function tests should be done before beginning pemoline therapy and periodically throughout treatment.

Neurotoxicity

In laboratory animals, some stimulants, especially methamphetamine, have shown neurotoxicity in high doses. This has never been demonstrated in humans, and has not been noted clinically in therapeutic doses, even though stimulants have been used for treatment of ADHD for 60 years.

Therapeutic Use of Nicotine

Tobacco use is significantly higher among adolescents and adults with ADHD than among non-ADHD peers. This observation led to a hypothesis that such persons were self-medicating because nicotine, a cholinergic agonist, indirectly stimulates the catecholamine system suspected to be deficient in ADHD. At least one controlled study in adults showed significant benefit from a nicotine patch,[36,37] which may be a viable treatment for adults already addicted to nicotine. In these patients, this therapy may prevent the respiratory complications of smoking, as well as benefit their ADHD symptoms. *However, it should not be used in children or in younger adolescents who are not already tobacco users, because it could unnecessarily induce addiction in some who otherwise might not have smoked.* A possible exception is comorbid Tourette's syndrome, which also benefits from nicotine, and which may be worsened by stimulants in some cases, restricting the therapeutic options. Nicotine is not a standard treatment for ADHD at this time.

Spurious Methylphenidate Liver Tumor Scare

Clinicians must know the facts about some misinformation that may still be circulating about methylphenidate and liver tumors in mice. The sensationalized version was that methylphenidate was found to cause liver tumors in laboratory mice. Although technically accurate, this incomplete version is misleading. The actual facts published in *Toxicology*[38] are these:

Rats and a strain of mice known to easily develop liver tumors were given methylphenidate, 4 to 67 mg/kg, each day for 2 years. There was no increase in tumors of any kind in the rats, and no increase in tumors in mice except for the liver tumors. Most of the increased mouse liver tumors were benign. Only in male mice at the highest dose did a small increase of hepatoblastoma, a malignant tumor, occur.

Table 4-6: Suggested Titration Schedule for Common ADHD Drugs

Most of these suggestions vary somewhat from FDA-approved package inserts. For most drugs (including stimulants), b.i.d. means AM and about noon; clonidine is an exception, as one of the doses should be given h.s.

Drug	Suggested Beginning Dose
Amphetamine SR spansules	5-10 mg q AM
Adderall XR™	10 mg q AM
Amphetamine tablets	2.5-5 mg b.i.d. or q AM*
Methylphenidate SR (racemic)	10-20 mg SR q AM
Methylphenidate (racemic) tabs**	5 mg b.i.d.
Concerta™ osmotic-release tabs	18 mg q AM
Pemoline	18.75-37.5 mg q AM
Imipramine Desipramine Amitriptyline	10 mg q AM or b.i.d.
Nortriptyline	10 mg q AM or b.i.d.

SR = slow release

* The FDA-approved package insert recommends starting dextroamphetamine with 2.5 mg q AM for preschoolers and increasing weekly by 2.5 mg/d; for 6 years and older, the recommendation is 5 mg q AM or b.i.d., increasing weekly by 5 mg/d. However, the effect of a given dose

Suggested Titration Increments (daily dose)	Suggested Adjustment Intervals	Usual Dosing
5 mg	2 days-1 week	5-30 mg q AM
10 mg	2 days-1 week	10-30 mg q AM
2.5-5 mg	2 days-1 week	2.5-10 b.i.d.-t.i.d.
10-20 mg	2 days-1 week	10-60 mg q AM-b.i.d
5 mg	2 days-1 week	2.5-20 mg t.i.d. (maybe q.i.d.)
18 mg	2 days-1 week	18-54 mg q AM
18.75 mg	weekly	18.75-75 mg q AM-b.i.d.
10-15 mg	weekly	b.i.d.-t.i.d.
10 mg	weekly	b.i.d.-t.i.d.

will be obvious within a day or two (usually within an hour), so that titration can be faster than weekly, barring side effects, which are less likely with slower titration.

** Doses for dextro-threo-methylphenidate, when it becomes available, will probably be half those for racemic threomethylphenidate.

(continued on next page)

Table 4-6: Suggested Titration Schedule for Common ADHD Drugs
(continued)

Drug	Suggested Beginning Dose
Bupropion	37.5 mg q AM or b.i.d.
Buspirone	5 mg b.i.d.-t.i.d.
Clonidine	0.05 mg b.i.d.
Guanfacine	0.5 mg h.s.
Haloperidol*	0.5 mg/d
Chlorpromazine*	10 mg q.d.-q.i.d.

* Neuroleptics such as haloperidol and chlorpromazine
  should be a last resort.

When human data were checked for hepatoblastoma, no evidence suggested an increase during the previous 15 years, while methylphenidate use multiplied during that time. Furthermore, hepatoblastoma, although rare, is more common in preschoolers, who are less likely to be treated with methylphenidate than are school-aged children. Dunnick and Hailey state that there is "no evidence of a carcinogenic effect in humans."[38] Furthermore, the rats taking methylphenidate showed a decrease in two kinds of tumors. In this regard, the rat data seem more like human experience than do the mouse data, for studies in humans[38]

Suggested Titration Increments (daily dose)	Suggested Adjustment Intervals	Usual Dosing
25-75 mg	1-2 weeks	37.5-150 mg b.i.d.
5 mg	1-2 weeks	10 mg b.i.d.-t.i.d.
0.05 mg	weekly	0.05-0.1 mg q.i.d.
0.5 mg	weekly	0.5-2 mg b.i.d.-t.i.d.***
0.5 mg	weekly	b.i.d-t.i.d.
10-25 mg	weekly	b.i.d.-q.i.d.

*** It may be useful to make the h.s. dose of guanfacine larger than the AM dose. Total daily dose generally does not exceed 3 to 4 mg.

report "a less than expected rate of cancers in patients taking methylphenidate"!

Importance of Titration: "Drill to Water, But Not Past It"

For most of the drugs in Table 4-1, the dosage ranges are so broad that a standard dose, even one based on mg/kg, is not feasible or good clinical practice. It is essential to begin low (Table 4-6) to prevent side effects and to make sure a low-dose therapeutic response is not missed in the occasional very sensitive patient or slow metabolizer ('don't drill past water'). It is equally important to titrate up as soon as the initial dose is confirmed ineffective. The minimum time between dose adjustments varies by half-life and other features of the drug, but a week is appropriate for most of the more common drugs. For example, a day or two is enough to observe the results of a given stimulant dose, but weekly intervals may be more convenient if the situation is not urgent. If it is not practical to have the patient return for each adjustment, some of the dose adjustments can be made by phone. In the case of school-aged patients, it is important to base the adjustment on information about both home and school functioning, including direct information from teachers, either by phone, fax, e-mail, or a note or rating scale given to the parents.[8]

Even for drugs expected to be administered b.i.d.-q.i.d., it is conservative, though not necessary, to start with a single morning dose on the first day to check for side effects and slow metabolism, then add the later dose(s) on the second day. The initial dose escalation can be quick for stimulants in the absence of side effects. For example, the prescription instruction can direct: "If no effect in 2 days, increase to . . . ." Suggested beginning doses for common drugs are shown in Table 4-6, and other suggestions about medicating are covered in Chapter 5.

References

1. National Institutes of Health. *Program and Abstracts of NIH Consensus Development Conference on Diagnosis and Treatment of ADHD.* Bethesda, MD, NIH, 1998, and NIH Consensus Statement: *Diagnosis and Treatment of ADHD.* Vol 16, No 2, Nov 16-18, 1998.

2. A 14-month randomized clinical trial of treatment strategies for attention-deficit/hyperactivity disorder (ADHD). The MTA Cooperative Group. *Arch Gen Psychiatry* 1999;56:1073-1086.

3. Moderators and mediators of treatment response for children with ADHD: the MTA study. The MTA Cooperative Group. *Arch Gen Psychiatry* 1999;56:1088-1096.

4. Taylor E: Development of clinical services for attention-deficit/hyperactivity disorder. *Arch Gen Psychiatry* 1999;56:1097-1099.

5. Greenhill LL, Halperin JM, Abikoff H: Stimulant medications. *J Am Acad Child Adolesc Psychiatry* 1999;38:503-512.

6. Geller B, Reising D, Leonard HL, et al: Critical review of tricyclic antidepressant use in children and adolescents. *J Am Acad Child Adolesc Psychiatry* 1999;38:513-516.

7. Diamond IR, Tannock R, Schachar RJ: Response to methylphenidate in children with ADHD and comorbid anxiety. *J Am Acad Child Adolesc Psychiatry* 1999;38:402-409.

8. Clinical practice guideline: treatment of the school-aged child with attention-deficit/hyperactivity disorder. *Pediatrics* 2001; 108:1033-1044.

9. Higgins ES: A comparative analysis of antidepressants and stimulants for the treatment of adults with attention-deficit hyperactivity disorder. *J Fam Pract* 1999;48:15-20.

10. Spencer T, Biederman J, Wilens T, et al: Pharmacotherapy of attention-deficit hyperactivity disorder across the life cycle. *J Am Acad Child Adolesc Psychiatry* 1996;35:409-432.

11. Wender PH: Pharmacotherapy of attention-deficit/hyperactivity disorder in adults. *J Clin Psychiatry* 1998;59:76-79.

12. Elia J, Borcherding BG, Rapoport JL, et al: Methylphenidate and dextroamphetamine treatments of hyperactivity: are there true nonresponders? *Psychiatry Res* 1991;36:141-155.

13. Sharp WS, Walter JM, Marsh WL, et al: ADHD in girls: clinical comparability of a research sample. *J Am Acad Child Adolesc Psychiatry* 1999;38:40-47.

14. Conners CK, Casat CD, Gualtieri CT, et al: Bupropion hydrochloride in attention deficit disorder with hyperactivity. *J Am Acad Child Adolesc Psychiatry* 1996;35:1314-1321.

15. Hunt RD, Capper L, O'Connell P: Clonidine in child and adolescent psychiatry. *J Child Adolesc Psychopharmacol* 1990;1:87-102.

16. Silva RR, Munoz DM, Alpert M: Carbamazepine use in children and adolescents with features of attention-deficit hyperactivity disorder: a meta-analysis. *J Am Acad Child Adolesc Psychiatry* 1996;35:352-358.

17. Spencer T, Biederman J, Wilens T, et al: Effectiveness and tolerability of tomoxetine in adults with attention deficit hyperactivity disorder. *Am J Psychiatry* 1999;155:693-695.

18. Arnold LE, Christopher J, Huestis R, et al: Methylphenidate vs dextroamphetamine vs caffeine in minimal brain dysfunction:

controlled comparison by placebo washout design with Bayes' analysis. *Arch Gen Psychiatry* 1978;35:463-473.

19. Arnold LE, Huestis RD, Smeltzer DJ, et al: Levoamphetamine vs dextroamphetamine in minimal brain dysfunction. Replication, time response, and differential effect by diagnostic group and family rating. *Arch Gen Psychiatry* 1976;33:292-301.

20. Arnold LE, Huestis RD, Wemmer D, et al: Differential effect of amphetamine optical isomers on Bender Gestalt performance of the minimally brain dysfunctioned. *J Learn Disabil* 1978;11:127-132.

21. Zametkin A, Rapoport JL, Murphy DL, et al: Treatment of hyperactive children with monoamine oxidase inhibitors. I. Clinical efficacy. *Arch Gen Psychiatry* 1985;42:962-966.

22. Spencer T, Biederman J, Harding M, et al: Growth deficits in ADHD children revisited: evidence for disorder-associated growth delays? *J Am Acad Child Adolesc Psychiatry* 1996;35:1460-1469.

23. Pelham WE, Aronoff HR, Midlam JK, et al: A comparison of Ritalin and Adderall: efficacy and time-course in children with attention-deficit/hyperactivity disorder. *Pediatrics* 1999;103:e43. Available at http://www.pediatrics.org/cgi/content/full/103/4 /e43. Accessed June 21, 1999.

24. Arnold LE: Methylphenidate vs amphetamine; a comparative review. *J Attention Disord* 2000;3(4):200-211.

25. Winkler J, Krim L, Marsh C: Improved Ritalin offers smaller doses and fewer side effects. Press release and presentation about dextro-threo-methylphenidate at American Chemical Society National Meeting, Anaheim, CA, March 22, 1999.

26. Conners CK: Controlled trial of methylphenidate in preschool children with minimal brain dysfunction. In: Gittelman R, Klein, eds. *Recent Advances in Child Psychopharmacology*. New York, Human Sciences Press, 1975.

27. Schleifer M, Weiss G, Cohen N, et al: Hyperactivity in preschoolers and the effect of methylphenidate. *Am J Orthopsychiatry* 1975;45:58-30.

28. Cohen NJ, Sullivan J, Minde K, et al: Evaluation of the relative effectiveness of methylphenidate and cognitive behavior modification in the treatment of kindergarten-aged hyperactive children. *J Abnorm Child Psychol* 1981;9:43-54.

29. Aman MG, Kern RA, McGhee DE, et al: Fenfluramine and methylphenidate in children with mental retardation and ADHD:

clinical and side effects. *J Am Acad Child Adolesc Psychiatry* 1993;32:851-859.

30. Klorman R, Brumaghim JT, Fitzpatrick PA, et al: Clinical effects of a controlled trial of methylphenidate on adolescents with ADD. *J Am Acad Child Adolesc Psychiatry* 1990;29(5):702-709.

31. Wilens TE, Spencer TJ, Swanson JM, et al: Combining methylphenidate and clonidine: a clinically sound medication option. *J Am Acad Child Adolesc Psychiatry* 1999;38:614-620.

32. Swanson JM, Flockhart D, Udrea D, et al: Clonidine in the treatment of ADHD: questions about safety and efficacy. *J Child Adolesc Psychopharmacol* 1995;5:301-304.

33. Swanson JM, Connor DF, Cantwell D: Combining methylphenidate and clonidine: ill-advised. *J Am Acad Child Adolesc Psychiatry* 1999;38:617-622.

34. Dech B: Clonidine and methylphenidate. *J Am Acad Adolesc Psychiatry* 1999;38:1469-1470.

35. Scahill L, Chappell PB, Kim YS, et al: A placebo-controlled study of guanfacine in the treatment of children with tic disorders and ADHD. *Am J Psychiatry* 2001;158:1067-1074.

36. Levin ED, Conners CK, Silva D, et al: Transdermal nicotine effects on attention. *Psychopharmacology (Berl)* 1998;140:135-141.

37. Conners CK, Levin ED, Sparrow E, et al: Nicotine and attention in adult attention deficit hyperactivity disorder (ADHD). *Psychopharmacol Bull* 1996;32:67-73.

38. Dunnick JK, Hailey JR: Experimental studies on the long-term effects of methylphenidate hydrochloride. *Toxicology* 1995;103:77-84.

Chapter 5

The Art of Medicating ADHD

T
he National Institute of Mental Health (NIMH) Multimodal Treatment Study of Children with ADHD (MTA) reported some interesting findings at the end of 14 months of treatment.[1,2] This six-site co-operative agreement study randomly assigned 579 children, ages 7 to 9, with well-diagnosed ADHD, combined type, to one of four treatment conditions: medication management, behavioral treatment, a combination of both, or community comparison. The first three groups were treated systematically by the MTA study for 14 months, and all groups were periodically reassessed. The community comparison subjects obtained whatever treatment they chose in the community, delivered in the routine manner by community providers.

Two thirds of the community comparison families obtained medication from their community provider during the 14 months that the other three groups were being treated by the MTA, and the medications were generally of the same type (mostly stimulants) as those given to the MTA-treated children, though at a slightly lower dose. However, 14-month outcomes in the two groups medicated systematically by the MTA significantly surpassed the outcomes of the community-comparison children for core ADHD symptoms, oppositional-aggressive behavior, and social skills.[2]

The advantage of the MTA medication management was not only statistically highly significant, but also clinically significant: on some measures, the effect size (ES) of the outcome difference between MTA medication management and community comparison was half of the effect sizes usually found between placebo and stimulant. Medication carefully managed by the MTA seemed almost twice as effective as the same drugs routinely used in the community. Thus, *how* the drugs are prescribed (including titration and dose management) may be as important as *whether* the drugs are prescribed. The art of medicating ADHD may be as important as the pharmacology of medicating ADHD.[3] Relevant strategies, most of which are also endorsed by the American Academy of Pediatrics Practice Guideline[4], are listed in Table 5-1. Most of this chapter is framed for pediatric patients, but the same principles apply with appropriate adjustments to adults with ADHD.

Presenting/Developing the Plan and Optimizing Placebo Effect

The initial presentation of treatment recommendations should address three related goals: (1) give the patient and family the necessary knowledge; (2) facilitate acceptance of the plan and future compliance; and (3) optimize placebo effect. The first two sometimes require drawing on the information in Chapters 1 and 4. All three goals can be promoted by actively involving the patient and family in development of the treatment plan (Chapters 3 and 8).

Necessary Information

In addition to explaining the nature of the diagnosis in a way that recognizes the seriousness of the disorder without setting up pessimistic expectations (Chapter 8), the clinician must describe specific expected effects of the recommended medication, including side effects, the expected duration of treatment, possible alterna-

Table 5-1: Salient Strategies in the Art of Medicating ADHD

Strategies	Reasons
Allow enough time for follow-up (at least 20-min appointments; MTA used 30 min)	Need time to do everything listed below
Careful initial titration	Maximize benefit/side effect ratio (see Chapter 4)*
Frequency of follow-up (weekly during titration, then 1 to 2 months)	Necessary for rational titration, maintain rapport/compliance, 'nip problems in bud'*
For child, direct information from teacher (fax, phone, rating scale, report card, e-mail)	Parent may not observe effect of medication, especially if it wears off by evening.*
Maximize placebo effect	Medication benefit is part pharmacologic, part placebo; for full benefit, need both

tives, and the targets of treatment. The clinician can frankly refer to the popular controversy about medicating ADHD and cite the scientific facts. The DEA Schedule II classification of stimulants must be addressed. In fact, it is advisable to warn the patient and/or family that the pharmacist may challenge them about the drug, and well-meaning but uninformed relatives or friends may be critical.

Strategies	Reasons
Minimize side effects by adjustments and preparation	Side effects reduce quality of life, lose rapport/compliance, remind patient she/he is sick.*
Cultivate rapport with patient and family	Necessary for compliance*
Some time alone with child at each visit	Rapport; facilitate compliance; learn about compliance lapses that parent doesn't know
Attention to structure, support, assisting transition of roles	Medication does not work in a vacuum; only makes possible, not automatic; need to facilitate human adjustment to and use of medication effect.
Prepare for long duration of treatment	Chronic disorder requires chronic treatment.*

* These strategies are also recommended by the American Academy of Pediatrics Practice Guideline.[4]

Facilitating Acceptance and Compliance

Although no clinician should attempt to 'sell' a patient or family on medication for ADHD, there is an ethical obligation to provide the facts to balance any misinformation from popular media. Citing the results of scientific studies in plain lay language permits a balanced, informed decision, which, if positive, forms a solid foundation for compliance. If the patient or family refuses medication, the clinician's accepting attitude, with a willingness to try other treatments, such as behavioral therapy (Chapter 6) or diets, keeps the door open for later acceptance by the patient or family if the alternatives do not suffice.

Importance of avoiding school-time dosing. A common compliance objection by school-aged children is that they do not want classmates to know they take medicine that brands them as 'hyper.' Taking medicine at school may also embroil them in school politics, with some educators and critics having passionate opinions about medication for ADHD. Generally, schools do not like to be responsible for administering medication and may pass the nuisance on to the child in various ways. Some schools openly remind children about their medication time in front of peers and staff, even using the public address system at times. While in an ideal world it should be possible to be so open without stigma, the current social realities make this experience quite uncomfortable for some children. Consequently, it is important to find a way to keep the medication between parent and child, with the school's only role being to provide periodic feedback on performance. Fortunately, good sustained-release stimulant preparations, such as once-daily Concerta™ (methylphenidate), Dexedrine® Spansule (amphetamine), and Adderall® XR, are now available to help avoid school-time doses, and additional long-action options are being prepared for market. (See *Time-Action Effects* later in this chapter). Most children show obvious relief when told they will not be taking medicine at school.

Optimizing the Placebo Effect

Every effective medication has two main benefits: pharmacologic and placebo. For maximal therapeutic effect, both components are desirable. Placebo effect is by far the safer component and, in some cases, the more powerful. It often starts working before the prescription is even filled, and in some cases is so satisfactory that the prescription remains unfilled, the pharmacologic component being unnecessary. In other cases, the prescription may be filled but not ingested, merely carried in a pocket or purse as a security measure, with good effect. A wise clinician does not scorn such clinical outcomes, but accepts them as evidence of a therapeutic tool.

Placebo effect can be variably defined as *vis medicatrix naturae* (healing power of nature), TLC (tender loving care) concretized into a pill, or the power of expectation (which has been demonstrated to affect the immune system and brain amines). It is a therapeutic phenomenon vested in the patient and family for the benefit of the patient, but strengthened or weakened by the clinician's handling of the issues in this chapter. One of the best ways to strengthen it is a matter-of-fact, though carefully worded, recital of the specific expected benefits and, paradoxically, expected side effects. The following example script uses a stimulant, the most common prescription for ADHD (and recommended by the American Academy of Pediatrics Practice Guideline[4]), and a child patient, the most common age, but the same principles apply to other drugs and other ages. It is not meant to be a memorized script, but an illustration that clinicians can adapt to their own style.

Example Script

"Fortunately, this disorder does respond to treatment. There are many different treatments; the best proven ones are medication such as stimulants and antidepressants, and behavioral treatments. Recent studies show that stimulants continue to provide benefit for several years and that they generally improve attention span, improve impulse control, and calm overactivity. While taking stimulants, children's social skills improve, they are more responsive to discipline, and their grades usually go up.

"There are some drawbacks, of course, that you need to know about. One is that there is a lot of variation from one person to another in the response to stimulants. One person might respond better to one, while somebody else responds better to another. Usually, two thirds of those trying one stimulant respond well; then two thirds of the others respond well to a different stimulant. Even among those who respond well to a given stimulant, the best dose can vary from 5 mg/d to 50 mg/d, and we don't have good ways to predict how much a particular person needs. Therefore, if you decide to try one, we'll start low and work up in dosage; we may have to try many different doses and possibly different drugs to find the best drug and dose for you.

"Any medicine strong enough to help is strong enough to have side effects. I want to tell you about them so that, if they occur, you'll know what they are and won't worry about them. They're generally more nuisance than danger. The most common are temporary loss of appetite and trouble getting to sleep at night. The appetite problem, as we know from people who have taken this medicine for diet, doesn't last, at least not in full force, and there are some ways to work around it in timing of meals and doses. The sleep problem can usually be handled by timing of the last dose and other things we'll talk about. Some children get a stomach ache for a few days until they get used to the medicine. It's also possible to get tics or worsening of tics—muscle twitches or sounds like throat clearing—and, if that becomes bothersome, it would be a reason to reduce the dose or try a different medicine.

"A few children get depressed, which is a sign of overdosage, and this improves when the dose is reduced. Some get overly quiet, and we could try adjusting the dose for that. Some may get a headache, which usually gets better as time goes on, but if it's too bad, we can reduce the dose or try a different medicine. There have been rare cases of hallucinations, such as seeing things or having sensations of skin crawling, which go away when the medicine is stopped or reduced. For the first 2 years of stimulant, there may be some growth slowing to about three fourths the usual rate of growth, but studies show that this catches up later. To make sure there is not a big problem with side effects, I'll want you to stay in close touch, especially while we're adjusting the dose to find the best one.

"One other thing I want to mention: stimulants, when taken as directed in usual doses, are medically safe enough that they might be over-the-counter drugs, like aspirin, if it were not for the fact that some adults get addicted to them (such as when taking them for diet). Because of the abuse problem, they are listed as Schedule II dangerous drugs by the Drug Enforcement Administration. There is no evidence that taking them for treatment of ADHD as a child leads to later abuse or addiction. However, you can expect that some well-meaning person, perhaps the pharmacist, will warn you about this being a 'dangerous drug,' so I wanted to forewarn you about it, so you're prepared."

Managing Side Effects

In the example, the side effects are presented with prepared plans for managing them. The plan is not only important in its own right, but also as reassurance to the patient and family that the side effects need not be feared. The side effects can even be used to set positive expectations: they show that the medicine is working. A patient who gets too quiet or even depressed may have too much of a good thing, and could use a dosage reduction. They are also valuable clues to time-action effects, showing the duration of action of a given dose in the particular patient.

Irritability is not a listed side effect in Table 5-2, despite the popular belief that it is a side effect of stimulants. Actually, irritability is a feature of ADHD, especially ADHD with comorbid oppositional-defiant, conduct, or mood disorder. It is usually suppressed by stimulants, but may manifest again each evening during the rebound as the medication wears off. Parents may report that a child is 'worse' or 'more irritable' in the evening, although much of this perception may be in contrast to the medicated state rather than to the state before medication. Rarely, mid-morning irritability may occur, which is a side effect that

113

Table 5-2: Managing Side Effects While Medicating ADHD

Most common side effects of stimulants improve with time.

Side Effect	Management Strategies, Techniques
Anorexia (stimulants)	Good breakfast immediately after (or before) AM dose; generous bedtime snack or late supper after stimulant wears off. Time meals/snacks during troughs just before next dose; possible sustained-release or different stimulant.
Sleep delay (stimulants)	Adjust time or size of last dose or switch from sustained-release to regular. Bedtime routine (quiet activity, story, warm milk, reward for being ready on time and staying in bed). If necessary: melatonin, diphenhydramine (Benadryl®), or trazodone (Desyrel®) in evening (some actually sleep better with an h.s. dose of stimulant). Possible switch to a different drug.
GI discomfort (mostly stimulants)	Lower dose temporarily; take medication with food. Assure time-limited 'until stomach gets used to it.' If necessary, switch to a different drug.
Blunting, 'zombie' affect (mostly stimulants)	Lower dose; evaluate for depression; reassure not inherently harmful; try different drug. Ultimately, may have to balance this cosmetic side effect against benefits.

Side Effect	Management Strategies, Techniques
Depression, suicide thoughts (rare)	Lower dose. Most who get depressed from a stimulant do well at a lower dose, with abatement of depression; not usually necessary to discontinue or switch drugs.
Evening 'rebound' of symptoms	Switch to sustained-release, or give small late afternoon (stimulants) dose to taper for the day.
Whining/crying, tearfulness, hypersensitivity (mainly stimulants)	Counsel parents that while child previously required stern discipline to get his/her attention, she/he is now more sensitive, and they can now switch to more gentle discipline. Temporary dose reductions.
Hallucinations (rare)	Reduce dose or discontinue stimulant, taper α_2-agonist. If hallucinations continue, start neuroleptic or refer to psychiatrist.
Seizures (very rare)	Discontinue current medication. If amphetamine not tried, switch to it. Consider carbamazepine or valproate (increase dose if already taking).
Somnolence, sedation	Reduce dose. For long-acting drugs, switch more of dose to late afternoon so sedative side effect wears off by next morning.

(continued on next page)

**Table 5-2:   Managing Side Effects
              While Medicating ADHD**
(continued)

Most common side effects of stimulants improve with time.

Side Effect	Management Strategies, Techniques
Dry mouth (TCAs, α_2-agonists)	Sips; chewing gum or lozenges (school more likely to allow lozenges/cough drops than gum—may need physician's note). If unusually severe, may need to decrease dose or switch medications.
Headaches	Dose reduction; acetaminophen or aspirin if needed. Monitor blood pressure, careful history to characterize headache: if hypertensive, switch med or add α_2-agonist; if migraine, add migraine treatment (eg, SSRI).
Tics (stimulants)	Reduce dose until patient gets used to medication, then, if needed, titrate slowly; consider switching drug. If methylphenidate not tried, switch to it. Check family history for Tourette's. Mild transient tics with no impairment may be tolerated in the risk/benefit ratio and may abate spontaneously despite continued medication.

requires dose reduction. The evening rebound of symptoms, if it occurs, usually lasts about an hour; it is desirable to anticipate it and structure the evening so that the child can be alone in some pleasant activity with no external demands for that hour. It can usually be lessened by manipulations of dose or dosage form to provide a daily taper.

Time-Action Effects of Stimulants

The following recommendations are not meant to imply that the clinical effect of stimulants correlates with blood levels across patients; there is no evidence for this, and laboratory blood tests have no demonstrated value for clinical monitoring of stimulants as they do for some other drugs. However, for a given patient, blood levels and clinical effect are influenced by size and timing of doses.

Most immediate-release stimulants, especially methylphenidate (Methylin™, Ritalin®), have a relatively short half-life (2 to 5 hours, depending on the drug), making the management of time-action effects critical. The goal is to maintain optimal effects during the waking hours, but to have the stimulant wear off in time to keep from interfering with sleep. (Paradoxically, some patients sleep better with a bedtime dose of stimulant, but this is not usually recommended.) Four critical issues are: the timing of doses and choice of dosage forms to get through the school day (with many children and schools preferring not to have medication administered at school); mealtimes; homework completion; and evening rebound/bedtime (Table 5-3).

Unfortunately, the longest-acting molecule, pemoline (Cylert®), has been demoted to a second-line choice because of liver toxicity. Furthermore, the traditional sustained-release form of methylphenidate often seems not to work or else fails to last through the school day, although sustained-release amphetamine seems more likely to suffice. Apparently, methylphenidate's rapid tachyphylaxis requires ever-changing blood levels for clinical effect, and the traditional slow-release form maintains a level that is too even. A new osmotic slow-release form using OROS®, recently marketed as Concerta™, solves this problem for some patients. Notably, Concerta™ was engineered to approximate the ascending blood level curve of t.i.d. methylphenidate, which was used in the highly successful MTA medication strategy. Thus, the same results can be obtained without the need for medication at school.

Table 5-3: Management of Time-Action Effects With Stimulants

Issue	Problems
Optimizing	Most immediate-release stimulants wear off by end of day, maybe before noon; many children and schools don't want administration at school.
Evening homework completion	Daytime stimulant may wear off by time of evening homework, causing great angst for child and parent, with repercussions the next day when homework is due.
Bedtime	If stimulant effect carries through bedtime, may delay sleep. If it wears off too abruptly, rebound may sour prebedtime atmosphere.
Mealtimes	Stimulant may suppress appetite at regular meal times, but then ravenous when wears off.

Another encouraging recent report found that 70% of a small sample could get through the school day on a morning dose of regular (not sustained-release) Adderall® if the dose was raised high enough.[5] Figure 5-1 helps in understanding this phenomenon. The systemic level of a drug can be kept above the therapeutically effective level longer in three ways: (1) longer half-life (choice of drug or sustained-release form); (2) second dose as the first one dips to the therapeutic level (eg, AM and noon doses); or (3) higher AM dose. The latter strategy is limited by the possibility of side effects at the peak level. Because the threshold for side effects varies among patients, the feasibility of the third option also varies among patients. A

Solutions

Try sustained-release forms or longer-action forms, such as Concerta™; give AM dose as late as possible before leaving home; higher AM dose (Figure 5-1); careful history about prenoon trough and adjust noon dose to earlier.

Schedule homework in afternoon while stimulant still effective; additional small dose late afternoon to carry through homework; reduce distractions during homework; if early riser, homework in AM after AM dose and breakfast.

Sustained-release in AM or at noon may come out just right for some. Sculpted t.i.d. or q.i.d. doses with later doses lower than preceding ones to taper. Daily bedtime rituals. As last resort, mild evening sedative p.r.n.

Allow child to eat later (or change meal times). Good breakfast before AM dose takes effect. Good bedtime snack. Counsel parents that child not just being oppositional.

further complication is that the rate of metabolism also varies among patients, so that the average half-lives usually quoted may be longer or shorter in certain patients. Therefore, an individualized strategy should be chosen for each patient, depending on rate of metabolism, side effect threshold, the acceptability and feasibility of a noon dose at school or work, and the efficacy of the sustained-release forms in the particular patient.

If the AM and noon doses are equal, there may be an additive effect of the noon-dose peak with the tail of the AM dose, pushing the effective dose higher in the afternoon. This can be desirable for several reasons. Patients with ADHD appear to deteriorate somewhat in the after-

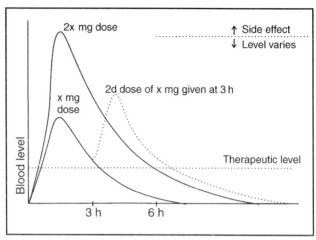

Figure 5-1: *Relationship of dosing strategy to clinical effect for drugs with short half-life. The systemic level can be kept above the therapeutic threshold through the school day or work day either by a second (and sometimes third) dose as the level drops, or by a higher initial dose, leading to a higher overall curve. The latter strategy can be used only if the patient's side effect threshold can tolerate the higher early peak.*

noon, requiring a higher effective dose. In the case of MPH, tachyphylaxis makes a higher blood level necessary for the same effect. However, in such a situation, afternoon-only side effects may occur. If the third dose is the same, the problem can be compounded further, setting the stage for an evening rebound. Therefore, it is often advisable to sculpt the doses, with the AM dose highest, and subsequent doses enough to keep the systemic level of drug rising slightly. Sometimes a third or fourth dose as low as 2.5 mg methylphenidate equivalent may work well to smooth the end of the day. Usually, most of these issues can be resolved by use of a morning dose of a good sustained-released formulation, such as Concerta™, Adderall® XR, or Dexedrine® Spansules, possibly supplemented by a small dose of immediate-release agent in the AM or late afternoon as needed.

References

1.　MTA Cooperative Group (1998). The Multimodal Treatment Study of Children with Attention-Deficit/Hyperactivity Disorder: 14-Month Outcomes, a special forum symposium at the 45th Annual Meeting of the American Academy of Child and Adolescent Psychiatry, Anaheim, CA, October 1998.

2.　A 14-month randomized clinical trial of treatment strategies for attention-deficit/hyperactivity disorder (ADHD). The MTA Cooperative Group. *Arch Gen Psychiatry*, 1999;56:1073-1086.

3.　Arnold LE: The art of medicating hyperkinetic children. *Clin Pediatr* 1973;12:35-41.

4.　Clinical practice guideline: treatment of the school-aged child with attention-deficit/hyperactivity disorder. *Pediatrics* 2001; 108:1033-1044.

5.　Pliszka SR, Browne RG, Wynne SK, et al: Comparing Adderall® and methylphenidate in ADHD. Presented at 152d Annual Meeting of American Psychiatric Association; May 19, 1999; Washington, DC. Abstract NR596.

Chapter **6**

Practical Behavioral Treatments

B ehavioral treatment is one of the two main treatments for ADHD, recommended by the American Academy of Pediatrics (AAP) Clinical Guideline[1] and documented by well-controlled, peer-reviewed studies as effective in most patients.[2-4] Although it is not generally as powerful as medication (the other well-documented treatment), it may be as good or better in some patients or certain situations, or may add to an unsatisfactory medication response (Table 6-1). Of particular interest is the ability of behavioral treatment to reduce the required dose of a medication for the same clinical benefit.[5-8] The therapeutic threshold—as depicted in Figure 5-1—is lowered by behavioral treatment, allowing lower doses to keep the pharmacologic curve above the critical threshold for optimal benefit. This feature may be crucial when a patient experiences a good medication response but with troublesome side effects at the optimal dose for symptom suppression.

There are as many different types of behavioral treatments as there are different drugs. They range from direct behavior modification through cognitive-behavioral strategies (such as teaching older children/adolescents and adults self-reinforcement) to training parents and teachers in the principles and application of social learn-

Table 6-1: When Behavioral Treatment (Tx) Is Especially Needed in ADHD*

Occasion for Behavioral Tx	Reason
Severe or complicated cases	Multiple problems need multiple-impact Tx. Severe problems need comprehensive approach.
Comorbidity, especially anxiety or depression	Some comorbidities not targeted by stimulants. Comorbidity worsens prognosis. Behavioral Tx effective for anxiety/depression even without medication.
When medication is declined	Behavioral Tx alone is viable alternative to medication for 75% of cases if intense enough.
When medication fails or is unsatisfactory on systematic, carefully titrated trials	Behavioral Tx is viable alternative to medication for 75% of cases if intense enough.
When medication is only partially satisfactory (eg, leaves secondary or comorbid symptoms)	Additive effect for non-core-ADHD symptoms and functional domains.
When optimal dose for behavior/learning causes side effects	Behavioral Tx lowers the dose for optimal effect, possibly below threshold for side effects.
When there are gaps in medication effect (eg, evenings)	Behavioral Tx effective any time of day.

* Although behavioral treatments (at least simple ones) are desirable for most cases, they are especially indicated for these situations.

Table 6-2: Behavioral Interventions Useful in ADHD

Intervention	Value
Daily report card	Closes gap between school and home, promoting parent-teacher-child cooperation. Proven effective for school behavior.
Clear rules and commands	Helps child organize self and schedule; reduces frustrated or confused antecedents of undesirable behavior.
Contingent attention (attend only to desired behaviors)	Powerful but nonaversive; improves parent-child relations.
Star charts targeted to desired behaviors	Simple, easy to understand, effective.
Home token economy	Gives parent behavior management leverage at any time, since points can be awarded or fined (at home or away); improves parent-child relations.
Time out	Humane aversive that prevents escalation of misbehavior.
Response cost	Humane aversive that is usually more effective than corporal punishment.

ing theory (Table 6-2). The implementation of behavioral treatment can range from keeping a simple star chart to establishing complex token economies at both home and school, integrated by structured communications, such as the daily report card.

Behavioral treatments can be sophisticated, with complex, labor-intensive interventions by psychologists, psychiatrists and other specialized mental health professionals; and some cases may require such a degree of sophistication. However, primary care clinicians can help many patients by implementing some simple interventions within the time constraints of daily practice. These interventions will become obvious once the following clinical 'nugget' is understood and practiced.

Behavioral Nugget

The following clinical nugget should guide the clinician and be imparted in some way to every parent of a child with ADHD. It can also be used by adults (and adolescents) in behavioral self-treatment. It is based on the basic principle that behavior is controlled by antecedents and consequences (the ABCs = antecedent, behavior, consequence). Antecedents elicit behaviors, and consequences determine their frequency of repetition. Consequences can be reinforcing (rewarding), extinguishing (neutral), or punishing (aversive). Behaviors that are reinforced, even intermittently, increase in frequency, while those that are not reinforced in some way (at least by self-satisfaction) decrease in frequency (extinguish). Punishment, if uncontaminated by reinforcement, accelerates the extinguishing of a behavior. However, the net result of punishment paired with reinforcement may be reinforcing, depending on the relative strengths of the reinforcer and aversive. This is one of the things that make punishment so tricky and often ineffective.

The most common reinforcing contaminant of punishment is *attention*. All reasonably normal humans naturally crave attention ("If you don't get stroked, your spinal cord will shrivel"—transactional analysis axiom). Attention is so reinforcing and the need for it so compelling that a person who cannot get positive attention will seek negative attention. A person who has no hope of gain-ing positive attention may even deliberately elicit negative attention in the form of punishment. Consequently, it is not unusual for troubled youngsters and their parents to be locked into a vicious cycle (Figure 6-1), in which the child's behavior is so disruptive that the parents are caught up in correcting it and have no time or energy left to give the child positive attention. Meanwhile, the child, despairing of getting the parents' approval, lives on what negative attention he or she can eke out. While this characterization is an extreme case, the following syllogism applies:

1. Behaviors that are reinforced increase in frequency.
2. Attention is a powerful reinforcer for most humans of all ages.
3. Therefore, *behavior to which attention is paid will increase in frequency.*[9]

The clinical lesson of this syllogism is that parents should pay attention to their child's desirable behavior (no matter how infrequent) and ignore undesirable behavior as much as possible. Part of the clinician's job is to convince parents to do so, through direct advice, explanation of the principle, and specific interventions. This job can be facilitated by referring the parent to an organized parent training group, such as the ones provided or sponsored by mental health clinics and parent support organizations like ChADD and ADDA. The more severe and challenging cases especially may need such support.

Star Charts

Star charts are daily records of a child's desirable behavior, recorded with some kind of positive mark, such as a star. One of the reasons star charts are so powerful, even though simple and easy, is that they focus attention on desired behavior, letting the corresponding undesirable behavior wither away from neglect. Therefore, to be most effective, star charts must state the goal in positive terms.

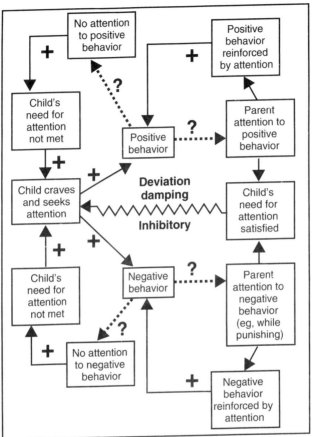

Figure 6-1: *Vicious cycle in which misbehavior is unwittingly reinforced by attention given during punishment. The misbehavior diverts parental efforts from attending to positive behaviors, so that the only attention the child can get is associated with punishment. The + signs mark arrows that are part of deviation-amplifying feedback loops. The jagged arrow indicates a damping or satisfying effect on the craving for attention. The 4 dotted arrows with ? indicate choice points for parents: pay attention to, or ignore, positive behavior or negative behavior.*

Thus, a star chart would record a child's dry nights and ignore enuretic ones, record the child's hanging up his or her coat and ignore when it is left lying on the floor, record when a child gets to bed on time and ignore resisted bedtimes, record homework completed on time and ignore neglected homework. Sometimes the additional reinforcement of a tangible reward is needed with a given star chart, but often, the attention and feeling of success are enough to increase the frequency of the targeted behavior. Remember that the clinician's attention is also important; so whenever a star chart is recommended, the family should be instructed to bring it back at the next visit, when the clinician should inquire about it and congratulate the child for any success, treating any failure matter-of-factly. To ensure that you remember to ask, make a note as part of the treatment plan.

Special Attention

Younger children can often benefit from 10 to 15 minutes several times a week of undivided attention from parent(s) in a special playtime. During this special time, the parent keeps up a running factual commentary on the child's activity, demonstrating that the parent is paying full attention, understands what the child is doing, and thinks it is important enough to note verbally. This tactic is especially useful when the parent-child interaction has been focused on the negative; it provides a 'sweeter' attention alternative to the 'sour' negative attention the child has been used to. Often, a parent has been so stressed by the child's undesirable behaviors that the only attention paid to the child is negative. Since everyone craves some attention, if the only attention is sour, the child will take it as the only kind available, perhaps deliberately eliciting it by further misbehavior. Thus, negative attention can reinforce the undesirable behavior it is meant to suppress (Figure 6-1). This vicious cycle can be broken by providing a more positive kind of attention. The child will prefer and begin to work for the positive attention once its availability is obvious.

Daily Report Card

The daily report card[10] (DRC) is a powerful intervention that can be as simple as having the teacher send a short note home each school day about how the child did that day, noting specific behaviors. A better version is to list certain target behaviors that the teacher can check off as present or not that day. There should not be more than 4 or 5 such behaviors, they should be chosen in consultation with the teacher, and they should be listed in a tabular checklist format (Figure 6-2). As with a star chart, behaviors should be stated positively, eg, *staying in seat unless excused* rather than *not running around the classroom.*

For maximum effect, successes on the DRC should be reinforced each day at home. One effective way to do this is by an individualized reward menu developed by the parents in consultation with the child (Figure 6-3), cooperatively deciding what reinforcers will be effective. However, the parents decide whether the rewards will be available on the menu. Things the child had been getting 'free' may be placed on the menu to be earned.

Token Economy

The reward menu for the DRC (Figure 6-3) could be refined into a home token economy by expanding the reward options and assigning a 'price' in points to be charged for each. In this case, it would be paired with a list of chores and other target behaviors for which points are awarded. The DRC could be folded into a token economy by awarding points for various success levels. Allowances can also be integrated with the token economy. Once established, a token economy allows an easy means of response cost—by taking away earned points through a system of fines for the resumption of undesirable behavior.

Daily Report Card			
Name: Jill	**Week of 2/22/2001**		
Target behavior	Through AM recess	From recess through lunch	Afternoon
Finish assignments	Y N	Y N	Y N
Remain seated except when excused	Y N	Y N	Y N
Keep hands and feet to self	Y N	Y N	Y N
Stay in line in corridor	Y N	Y N	Y N
Wait to be called on (instead of blurting answer)	Y N	Y N	Y N
Total Y =	_____		

Figure 6-2: Sample daily report card (DRC). The child's successes are reinforced by home rewards (See also Figure 6-3).

Response Cost and Time Out

Although the best way to get rid of undesirable behaviors is to crowd them out by increasing desirable behaviors, some behaviors are so dangerous, disruptive, or bothersome that active suppression is needed. *Response cost* means that it costs the child something for engaging in a

Reward menu for Jill		
List A *Choose one for 10 yeses*	**List B** *Choose one for 12 yeses*	**List C** *Choose one for 14 yeses*
• 15 min TV	• 2 of list A items	• 3 of list A
• 15 min Nintendo	• 30 min TV	• 1 of list A + 1 of list B
• Ice cream for bedtime snack	• 30 min Nintendo	• 30 min game with Dad
• Pastry snack in lunch next day	• 15 min game with Dad	• Ice cream for supper and bedtime snack
	• Stay up 15 min later	• Have friend over for an hour

Bonus for 5 days with 14 yeses each:
Trip to McDonald's

Figure 6-3: Sample reward menu for daily report card with 15 possible yeses.

certain behavior (response). Besides fines in the home token economy, other response costs might be fines against
allowance, depriving the child of a privilege or expected
dessert, grounding, or being left with a sitter while the rest
of the family enjoys some previously planned activity at
which the undesirable behavior would be inappropriate.

Time out also often involves some incidental response
cost, because a child in time out loses the opportunity for
reinforcing activities. As little attention as possible should
be given to a child in time out. To this end, the time out
area should be away from other people, and implementation should be as mechanical as possible, such as
with a timer, eliminating the need for talking. The area

Table 6-3: Troubleshooting a Behavioral Plan

Problems	Possible Causes
Child not interested in reinforcers	Wrong reinforcers Child getting reinforcers without earning them Child sated by earning too easily
Child interested in reinforcer but does not try to earn	No hope of earning; despair of success. Hoop set too high
Program worked at first, but stopped working	Satiation Parents no longer delivering the reinforcement Outgrowing of reinforcer
Child begs and whines for reinforcer	Parents not giving reinforcer when earned Parents giving in to begging, thereby reinforcing begging. Child hopeless about earning reinforcer or assumes easier to beg for it than earn it.
Target behaviors improve, but other behaviors worsen	Child thinks only the targets count, puts all effort into those.
Targets improve, but parents dissatisfied, more concerned about other behaviors	Wrong targets picked in the first place Parents perfectionists
Child demands reinforcers for behavior previously mastered	Natural opportunism of childhood

Adjustments Needed

Get child's help picking reinforcers; use preferred
activities as reinforcers.
Close loopholes in 'welfare system'; lock cupboards
if necessary.
Raise requirement for earning reinforcer.

Lower the hoop. Find a level that the child can succeed
at, then gradually raise requirement.

New reinforcers or raise requirement for earning the old ones.
Resume reinforcement, starting by giving 'back pay.'

Change reinforcers (with child's consultation).

Give back pay and keep 'wages' current.
Ignore begging after one explanation of how to earn the
reinforcer. Response cost or time out if necessary.
Lower requirement for earning so it is easier than begging;
make sure child knows begging won't work.

Add new targets covering new problem behaviors, with
reduced reinforcement for old targets; continued success on old
targets is required to be eligible for reinforcement on the new.

Reprioritize behavioral targets, stressing that the strategy is to
work on a few at a time, then add others as the new behaviors
become second nature.

Counsel parents about realistic expectations

Firmly explain that additional reinforcers will not be available
for established behavior, but continuing good behaviors is
necessary for earning reinforcement on the current targets.
Additional reinforcement might be earned by targeting
additional behaviors

must be devoid of enjoyable stimuli and activities. The time should be 2 to 15 minutes, depending on the child's age: 2 minutes for bright, older toddlers, 2 to 4 minutes for preschoolers, 5 minutes for elementary school age, 10 minutes for middle school. A rough rule of thumb might be mental age minus 2 for the number of minutes. The timer can be reset if the child has not settled down by the time it goes off. Sometimes, time out needs to be physically enforced, perhaps by locking a door. Alternately, the child might earn a shorter time by going to time out voluntarily and immediately settling down. Time out will not work well unless some positive attention is available. It is not appropriate for younger toddlers who do not understand, and mid- to late adolescents are usually better managed in other ways.

Clear Rules and Commands/Instructions

This is the only intervention in this chapter that directly addresses the role of antecedents in determining behavior. One of the reasons for much of the undesirable behavior of patients with ADHD is confused and disorganized frustration. Patients with ADHD have trouble structuring and organizing things for themselves, and have trouble reaching closure on vague instructions that most people would be able to figure out and carry out. They are often quite willing to do what is expected once they understand it, but they get frustrated and irritated when forced to guess or when given the latitude of doubt.

Therefore, parents should be encouraged to frame clear, unequivocal house rules (simple and not more than a total of 5 to 10) that govern general conduct. These rules should be posted in a prominent place, such as bulletin board or refrigerator. For children who do not yet read, pictures can be used to represent the rules. Examples of rules might be: always knock before entering another's room; do not use another's things without permission; or television viewing is allowed only between

Table 6-4: Bibliotherapy Readings: Some Books Parents and Children Have Found Useful

About ADHD:

ADD Quick Tips: Practical Ways to Manage Attention Deficit Disorder Successfully, by Carla Crutsinger and Debra Moore. Brainworks, Inc., 1918 Walnut Plaza, Carrollton, TX 75006-5856. Telephone: 972-416-9410.

Dr. Larry Silver's Advice to Parents on Attention-Deficit Hyperactivity Disorder, by Larry Silver. American Psychiatric Press, Washington, DC.

Teenagers with ADD: A Parent's Guide, by Dendy, Chris A. Zeigler. Woodbine House, Bethesda, MD, 1995. Telephone: 1-800-843-7323

All About ADHD: The Complete Practical Guide for Classroom Teachers, by Linda J. Pfiffner. Scholastic Professional Books, New York, 1996. Scholastic Professional Books, PO Box 7502, Jefferson City, MO. 65102. Telephone: 1-800-325-6149.

Teaching the Tiger. Hope Press. Helpful for parents trying to help with school learning and behavior problems. Summary available at http://hopepress.com.hopepres.html

About Normal Family Life and Adolescent Development:

Parents and Adolescents Living Together Part 1: The Basics, by G Patterson, M Forgatch. Eugene, OR Castalia Publishing Co, 1987.

Parents and Adolescents Living Together Part 2: Family Problem Solving, by G Patterson, M Forgatch. Eugene, OR Castalia Publishing Co, 1987.

Parents' Survival Handbook, by L. Eugene Arnold. LAMMP Publishing Co, 1983. Available through Steve Ramsey Associates, 28100 Cavallo Rd., Danville, OH 43014, Telephone: 740-599-5163. Common sense and applied science about growing up with your children.

7 and 9 PM. The consequences for following or violating the rules must also be clear.

Commands and instructions should be clear and specific, and issued only one or two at a time unless the child has demonstrated the ability to carry out longer sequences of instructions. No command should be given that the parent is not willing to go the last mile to enforce. Unenforced commands train the child to ignore commands. Better to give one command a day and enforce it than to give 10 commands and enforce five, allowing the child to disregard the other five.

Troubleshooting a Behavioral Plan

Just as medication dosage and timing need to be adjusted periodically, especially in the beginning (titration), a behavioral plan needs to be monitored and occasionally adjusted, especially in the beginning. Table 6-3 lists the most common problems and appropriate adjustments.

Other Interventions

In addition to the strictly defined behavioral treatments, attention to the psychosocial aspects of psychopharmacology is also useful. In the six-site NIMH Multimodal Treatment Study of ADHD (MTA), several differences existed between the significantly superior MTA medication management and routine community medication besides dose titration, thrice-daily methylphenidate, and medication 7 days a week.[8,11] One of the differences was that during the MTA monthly 30-minute medication visits, the pharmacotherapists were encouraged to provide (when indicated) empathetic support, reflection, clarifying questions, encouragement, and practical advice. Another feature of the MTA medication management program was the availability of informational and instructional readings[12] provided to parents as indicated or requested. Table 6-4 lists examples of such readings (although not the list used in the MTA treatment).

References

1.   Clinical practice guideline: treatment of the school-aged child with attention-deficit/hyperactivity disorder. *Pediatrics* 2001; 108:1033-1044.

2.   National Institutes of Health. *Program and Abstracts of NIH Consensus Development Conference on Diagnosis and Treatment of ADHD.* Bethesda, MD, NIH, 1998.

3.   Pelham WE, Wheeler T, Chronis A: Empirically supported psychosocial treatments for attention-deficit/hyperactivity disorder. *J Clin Child Psychol* 1998;27:190-205.

4.   Zametkin AJ, Ernst M: Problems in the management of attention-deficit/hyperactivity disorder. *N Engl J Med* 1999;340:40-46.

5.   Pelham WE, Schedler RW, Bender M, et al: The combination of behavior therapy and methylphenidate in the treatment of attention-deficit disorder: a therapy outcome study. In: Bloomingdale L, ed. *Attention Deficit Disorder.* Oxford (UK), Pergamon Press, 1988, Vol. 3.

6.   Horn WF, Ialongo NS, Pascoe JM, et al: Additive effects of psychostimulants, parent training, and self-control therapy with ADHD children. *J Am Acad Child & Adolesc Psychiatry* 1991;30: 233-240.

7.   Jensen PS, Payne JD: Behavioral and medication treatments for attention-deficit/hyperactivity disorder: comparisons and combinations. In: *Program and Abstracts of NIH Consensus Development Conference on Diagnosis and Treatment of ADHD.* Bethesda, MD, National Institutes of Health, 1998.

8.   A 14-month randomized clinical trial of treatment strategies for attention-deficit/hyperactivity disorder (ADHD). The MTA Cooperative Group. *Arch Gen Psychiatry* 1999;56:1073-1086.

9.   Arnold LE, ed. *Helping Parents Help Their Children: A Handbook for Professionals Who Guide Parents.* New York, Brunner/ Mazel, 1978.

10. O'Leary KD, Pelham WE, Rosenbaum A, et al: Behavioral treatment of hyperkinetic children: an experimental evaluation of its usefulness. *Clin Pediatr* 1976;15:510-515.

11. Arnold LE, Abikoff HB, Cantwell DP, et al: NIMH Collaborative Multimodal Treatment Study of Children With ADHD (MTA): design, methodology, and protocol evolution. *J Attention Disord* 1997;2:141-158.

12. Long N, Rickert VI, Ashcraft EW: Bibliotherapy as an adjunct to stimulant medication in the treatment of attention-deficit/hyperactivity disorder. *J Pediatr Health Care* 1993;7:82-88.

Chapter 7

Other Treatments for ADHD

Besides the well-established medications (Chapter 4) and behavioral treatments (Chapter 6), at least two dozen other treatments have been proposed for treating ADHD. These range in scientific documentation from successful, well-controlled, randomized clinical trials to promising pilot data, to mere hypotheses, to failure in controlled studies (Table 7-1). For example, elimination diets (Feingold, oligoantigenic, Few Foods) have a degree of documentation in properly selected subgroups that is as good as some drugs and behavioral techniques. On the other hand, three controlled studies of multivitamin megadosage therapies have failed to find efficacy for ADHD. Since a variety of groups zealously advocate many alternative treatments, evidence-based clinicians need to be conversant with the data to respond helpfully to questions from patients and their families. Furthermore, some alternative treatments could be useful adjuncts to standard clinical care, at least in selected cases. The following are highlights from a review of 'alternative treatments' for ADHD compiled for the November 1998 NIH Consensus Development Conference. Detailed referencing can be found in the published review.[1-3]

Table 7-1: Scientific Status of Treatment Alternatives for ADHD

Treatment	Etiology or Mechanism
Sympathomimetic stimulants	catecholamine, especially dopamine
Antidepressants and other psychotropics	catecholamine, serotonin
Behavioral Tx: behavior modification, contingency	social learning theory, shaping
Few Foods diet (oligoantigenic)	food or additive sensitivity
Enzyme-potentiated desensitization	food or additive sensitivity
Elimination of sugar alone	sugar malaise
Amino acid supplementation	precursors of catecholamines, serotonin
Essential fatty acid supplementation	prostaglandins neural membrane
L-carnitine	promotes EFA metabolism
Glyconutritional supplementation	need for glycoconjugates
Dimethylaminoethanol (DMAE)	acetylcholine precursor?

Type of Data; ES or *P*	Rating* (0-6)	Risks
>100 placebo XOs and RCTs in 1000s; ES 0.7-1.8, *P* = 0.01-0.001	6	side effects; doubt neurotoxic
multiple placebo-controlled RCTs; ES 0.5-1.5, *P* = 0.05-0.005	6	cardiotoxicity, other side effects
ABAB, random wait list controls; ES 0.5-1.2, *P* = 0.05-0.005	5-6	nuisance, time, labor-intensive expensive
controlled trial; placebo challenges; ES 0.5-1.0, *P*= 0.05-0.001	5	nuisance, expensive, nutrition
controlled comparison to placebo injections; *P* = 0.001	4	injection
placebo-controlled challenges; *P* >0.1	0	delay standard Tx
placebo-controlled comparisons; ES up to 0.6, *P* = 0.01	0	eosinophilia, neurotoxicity
serum level cf control placebo-controlled trials; ES 0.5, 0.1> *P* >0.05	3	upsetting balance
placebo trial other D/O, not ADHD. ES >2, *P* < 0.05	2	upsetting balance
open trials, 2 positive, 1 negative	0	upsetting balance
many open +DB trials, most poor ES 0.1-0.6, 0.1>*P*>0.05	3	modest effect, SE, expensive

(continued on next page)

Table 7-1: Scientific Status of Treatment Alternatives for ADHD (continued)

Treatment	Etiology or Mechanism
Vitamins	deficiency vs idiopathic need for higher dose
Iron supplementation	co-factor to make catecholamines
Zinc supplementation	co-factor for many enzymes
Magnesium supplementation	deficiency compared to controls
Chinese herbals	clinical experience
Other herbals	clinical experience
Homeopathic prep	clinical experience
Laser acupuncture	stimulate foci for calming
EEG biofeedback	suppress theta, increase beta
EMG biofeedback, relaxation training	lower arousal, muscle tone
Meditation	autonomic effect focused attention
Hypnosis	lower arousal

Type of Data; ES or P	Rating* (0-6)	Risks
placebo-controlled trials megavitamin combo, not RDA; megadose combo no benefit	0 1 for RDA, specific megavitamin	hepatotoxicity, neuropathy in megadose
open trial supplementation; ES 1.0, P <0.05	3 **	hemochromatosis from excess
compare zinc level of ADHD to control; ES 2.4, P <0.001	2 **	WBC aplasia from excess
open trial with control group; ES 1.2-1.4, P < 0.05	3 **	aggression from excess
open trials, one with MPH control; P < 0.05; no diff. from MPH	3	delay of other Tx
no data	1	delay of other Tx
no data	1	delay of other Tx
open trial; ES 1.0	2	delay other Tx, burn from laser
open and randomized wait list control trials; P < 0.05	3	expense, time
randomized trials with controls; ES 1.0-1.3, P < 0.01	4 for EMG/ relaxation	delay other Tx
comparison to relaxation, wait list control, med; P < 0.05	3	delay other Tx
hard to hypnotize	0	delay other Tx

(continued on next page)

Table 7-1: Scientific Status of Treatment Alternatives for ADHD (continued)

Treatment	Etiology or Mechanism
Mirror feedback	improve deficient self-awareness
Channel-specific perceptual training	basic readiness skills, focus
Vestibular stimulation	modulate behavior, attention, perception
Massage	muscular soothing, 5HT
Antifungal Tx	GI yeast toxin; breach mucosa
Thyroid Tx	thyroid function affects AD symptoms
Deleading	lead toxicity causes AD Sx

*Ratings: 0 = not worth considering further (despite, in the case of amino acids, some evidence of short-lived effect); 1 = credible hypothesis or collateral support or wide clinical experience, needs pilot data; 2 = promising systematic data, but not prospective trial; 3 = promising prospective data (perhaps with random assignment to control or objective/blind measures) lacking some important control, or controlled trial(s) with trends suggesting further exploration; 4 = one significant double-blind controlled trial needing replication, or multiple positive controlled trials in a treatment not easily blinded; 5 = convincing double-blind controlled evidence but needs further refinement (eg, define target subgroup) for clinical application ; 6 = should be considered established Tx for the appropriate subgroup.

**The rating would be 6 for patients showing frank deficiency of vitamins, iron, zinc, or other nutrients.

Type of Data; ES or P	Rating* (0-6)	Risks
randomized X-over w/ and w/o, cf. controls; ES 0.5, $P < 0.05$	3	may impair non-ADHD children
randomized prev trial with 2 control groups; ES 0.9, $P < 0.01$	3	delay other Tx
open and single-blind trials; ES 0.4-1.2, P = n.s. to 0.001	3	nausea accident
Single-blind comparison to relaxation. ES med-lg, $p<0.05$	3	negligible, bruise if too hard
no data in ADHD; other placebo trials; (ES 1.1-3, $P < 0.003$)	1	medication risk
placebo trial: 5/8 GRTH, 1/9 other; n.s. if thyroid normal	0 if thyroid normal; 6 if thyroid abnormal	thyroid toxicity
placebo-ctrl trial of chelation (=MPH); ES 0.7-1.6, P= 0.05-0.001	4 if blood Pb>20; 2 if Pb<20	toxicity of chelator

ES = effect size, Cohen's d (number of standard deviations difference in means); An effect size of 1.0 ('large') means that a patient receiving the treatment has an 80% chance of doing better than one not receiving the treatment; an effect size of 0 means the chance of improvement is equal between the treatment and the control condition. P = probability.

This table is adapted with permission from Arnold LE: Treatment alternatives for attention-deficit/hyperactivity disorder (ADHD). *J Attention Dis* 1999;3: 30-48, and Arnold LE: Treatment alternatives for attention-deficit/hyperactivity disorder. In: Jensen PS, Cooper J, eds. *Diagnosis and Treatment of ADHD: An Evidence-Based Approach.* Washington, DC, American Psychological Press, 2001. In press.

General Principles

1. Alternative treatments vary widely in efficacy, risk, expense, degree of scientific documentation, and, especially, in appropriate target patients, and cannot be lumped for evaluation.

2. Many alternative treatments are cause-targeted, in contrast to the palliative efficacy of the established treatments.

3. Being targeted to causes, many of the alternative treatments apply only to a small subgroup of ADHD patients. However, because ADHD is so prevalent, even a small percentage translates into a considerable number of patients. Furthermore, these might be patients who are unresponsive or only partially responsive to established treatments.

4. Sometimes a double standard of evaluation exists, in which a new drug may be accepted by clinicians for treatment of ADHD on the basis of a small open trial or even a report of chart review (presumably pending a controlled trial), but similar evidence is dismissed for an alternative treatment as being uncontrolled for placebo effect. Even a small placebo-controlled trial may be dismissed. Evidence-based clinicians should apply even-handed evaluations to all treatments. It is as unscientific to reject a treatment without evaluation as it is to accept it without evaluation. An even-handed scientific evaluation also sets a good example for the lay public, some of whom are quick to embrace new treatments uncritically.

5. Although alternative treatments are not necessarily safer than standard treatments, their main risk seems to be delaying standard treatment if the alternatives do not work. This seems to be an acceptable risk for a chronic disorder, in which a few weeks' delay of treatment should not usually be critical. Also, many alternative treatments can be used as adjuncts without delaying standard treatment.

Elimination Diets

Contrary to widespread clinical belief, elimination diets have good scientific support from double-blind, placebo trials in 5 countries on 3 continents.[3,4] The earlier, more equivocal trials seem to have suffered from unselective subject recruitment and failure to eliminate a broad enough spectrum of foods. The best-supported approach now is a Few Foods or oligoantigenic diet (Table 7-2), especially when used in middle-class preschoolers with ADHD, irritability, somatic symptoms, sleep disturbance, and history of atopy. However, favorable results have also been reported in older children. It is not clear what percentage of children with ADHD would be significantly helped by such a diet, but an educated guess, not based on data, would be 5% to 15%. An unpublished epidemiologic sample suggested that up to 30% of 3-year-olds benefit. The main disadvantages are compliance, nuisance, expense, possible parent-child conflicts about compliance, and delay of other treatments if the diet does not work.

If such a diet is undertaken, a 1 to 2 week trial should indicate whether there is enough benefit to continue. If so, then the patient should be challenged with one food component at a time to discover which foods are problematic for him or her. Sometimes the problem foods can be detected on skin testing. Enzyme-potentiated desensitization was reported useful in a placebo-controlled study; where available, this might substitute for the dietary eliminations. There is little or no evidence of a behavioral benefit from sugar restriction alone, despite repeated controlled trials.

Nutritional Supplements

All patients should have their nutritional status evaluated by diet history and examination, with laboratory tests where indicated. When a deficiency is found, it should be treated in a routine, conservative manner. A patient with a junk-food diet who is unwilling to change might benefit—at least in general health—from an RDA multivitamin.

Table 7-2: Example of Few Foods Diet

These are the only foods allowed for the initial trial. If successful, others can be added one at a time as 'challenges' to find the food(s) to which the patient is sensitive.

Lamb	Celery
Chicken	Carrots
Potatoes	Parsnips
Rice	Salt
Bananas	Pepper
Apples	Calcium
Cucumbers	Vitamins

Brassica (cabbage, cauliflower, broccoli, brussel sprouts)

However, no good evidence exists for long-term efficacy of amino acids or multivitamin megadosage therapies in ADHD, despite repeated controlled trials. Dimethylaminoethanol (DMAE, deanol) had numerous placebo-controlled studies that resulted in an FDA verdict of 'possibly effective.' Essential fatty acids, phospholipids, most minerals, and glyconutritional supplements must be considered unproven except for cases of demonstrated deficiency. One small study suggests that sufficient zinc nutrition may be important to achieve full benefit from stimulant medication.[5]

Herbals and Proprietaries

Good pilot data support some Chinese herbals, such as yizhi and Tiaoshen liquor,[6,7] but not Western herbals for ADHD. For example, hypericum (St. John's wort) is commonly used for treatment of ADHD in Europe, where stimulants are avoided. This is not unexpected because hypericum has a mild antidepressant effect, and many other antidepressants have been shown efficacious in ADHD. However, a literature search turned up no published data supporting such use. Herbal treatment is essentially primitive psychopharmacology, and while it is likely that some herbs can be useful, we cannot draw conclusions for most of them because systematically collected data are lacking. The same lack of data pertains to homeopathic and other proprietaries. Interestingly, one purveyor of Pycnogenol®, on the basis of open clinical experience, has stopped recommending it for ADHD. Some herbals, such as ephedrine, might be contraindicated.

EEG Biofeedback

Electroencephalographic (EEG) biofeedback is a theory-driven treatment. It is based on observations that some ADHD patients, when monitored on quantitative EEG, have excess theta-band power and low beta-band (above 12 Hertz) power, and that beta-band sensorimotor rhythm (12 to 15 Hertz) is associated with immobility in animals. A theoretical gap is the failure to consider caudate nuclei and other deep structures (EEG measures only surface cortical activity). Promising pilot data suggest that training the EEG more predominantly to the beta-band can improve behavior and learning. However, most of the data are from open trials, with no sham or placebo control, although one study had random assignment to feedback or wait list. Another study used a single-subject crossover design on four subjects selected for low arousal out of 12 candidates; three of these improved during real training and relapsed when the training was reversed; it is not clear whether this was a success rate of 75% (3 out of 4) or 25% (3 out of 12). When appropriately controlled studies of sufficient size are completed, EEG biofeedback may be found effective, possibly even a preferred treatment, for a subgroup of patients with ADHD (probably those with low arousal level and slow EEG). Until then, it must be considered an expensive experimental treatment.

Electromyographic Biofeedback, Relaxation Training, and Meditation

These three modalities all target relaxation, but use different strategies to achieve it. EMG biofeedback and relaxation training are commonly used together and may be synergistic. Randomized, controlled studies have demonstrated significant benefit from the combination, which is fairly quick, inexpensive, and of minimal risk. It may be especially useful for adolescents and adults with ADHD, who often complain of a restless feeling. Meditation indirectly achieves relaxation by focusing the mind on a nonarousing thought. It has some promising pilot data, including one favorable comparison to medication.

Mirror Feedback

Mirrors have been proposed as a way of increasing self-control and attentional focus by increasing self-focus in patients with ADHD.[8] Mirror feedback may eventually be found to be a useful adjunct to medication, helping with evening homework after the daytime dose wears off, or with office desk work for adults. In a single-blind, randomized trial, a word puzzle that differentiated hyperactive-impulsive (HI) patients from normal controls with an effect size (ES) of 0.75 ($P<0.05$) in the no-mirror condition showed a between-groups ES of only 0.2 (not significant) with a mirror in front of the child as he or she worked. The mirror improved the performance of the HI children by half the no-mirror difference between groups. The HI children who actually looked in the mirror equaled the no-mirror scores of the controls. This intervention carries a risk associated with diagnostic validity: the normal controls showed a trend of performance decrement with the mirror, especially if they looked in it.[8] Therefore, this technique should not be recommended unless the clinician is sure of the diagnosis.

Vestibular Stimulation

Two pilot studies (small but sham-controlled) suggest mild benefit—about half the effect of stimulants—from systematic stimulation of the semicircular canals by rotary stimulation. The benefit is probably confined to younger children. There is some risk of nausea, minimized if the child controls the stimulation. The technique can be done for toddlers/preschoolers on a sit-and-spin toy, and for older children on a swivel chair. Children often spontaneously tilt their heads in the right plane to stimulate semicircular canals optimally, but may need instruction in this (45 degrees forward in midline and to each side for the three pairs of canals). Though not a proven, established treatment, this may be worth a try, especially in toddlers or preschoolers for whom one wishes to delay medication.

Massage

The tactile and deep pressure stimulation of massage has a calming effect in many species of mammals.[9] In controlled studies, it increased serotonin levels and enhanced immune function.[10,11] A randomized controlled trial of 10 15-minute massage sessions compared with an equal amount of relaxation training in adolescents with ADHD showed significant superiority of massage on teacher hyperactivity ratings and time spent on task (77% vs 51%).[12] The massage consisted of 30 moderate-pressure, back-and-forth strokes in each of three areas: neck, neck to shoulder, and vertebral column neck to waist. Some occupational therapists substitute rolling a semihard rubber ball (such as a tennis ball) with moderate pressure in the same areas. This is a supplementary treatment that parents might be taught to carry out, and should be applicable to all age groups.

PANDAS and Immune Therapy

Pediatric autoimmune neuropsychiatric disorder associated with group A *Streptococcus* (PANDAS) generally involves tics and obsessive-compulsive disorder, but may carry a 40% rate of ADHD. Immune therapy is being explored as a possible treatment, presumably after eradication of the infection.

Antifungal Treatment

Children with ADHD have been reported to have histories of more upper respiratory infections and more antibiotic treatment than non-ADHD controls.[13] However, the antibiotics themselves can cause a yeast overgrowth, especially with a high-sugar diet (documented in animal studies),[14] with breakdown of gut mucosa allowing food allergens to be absorbed, as well as direct yeast neurotoxicity. Despite encouraging pilot results of antifungal therapy in candidiasis hypersensitivity with depression and premenstrual tension,[15] it remains an untested hypothesis for ADHD.

Helping Families To Be Sensible About Alternatives

To guide patients and their families through controversial claims about alternative treatments, the clinician must keep balanced and remain open to new information, especially data-based information. Unfortunately, zealous pseudoscience (eg, anecdotal testimony presented as evidence of efficacy) can be found among advocates of some treatments. However, this does not prove a treatment is ineffective, only that it is unproven scientifically. Every treatment, including medication, must be tested before it can be considered effective. Just as many molecules may be screened to find one effective drug, it is likely that many alternative treatments will need to be screened to find those that are effective. Neither blanket rejection nor uncritical blanket acceptance is useful.

Because patients or families often try alternative treatments on their own, a comprehensive clinician should be able to discuss them with the family. In particular, any risks of the treatment should be explained in realistic terms. The scientific evidence for efficacy is also useful information, allowing the patient or family to judge whether the possible benefit is worth the expense and risk. For some patients, a photocopy of Table 7-1 may be useful.

References

1.   Arnold LE: Treatment alternatives for attention-deficit/hyperactivity disorder (ADHD). *J Attention Dis* 1999;3:30-48.

2.   Arnold LE: Treatment alternatives for adults with ADHD. In: Wasserstein J, Wolfe LE, Lefever FF, eds. *Adult Attention-Deficit Disorders: Brain Mechanisms and Life Outcomes*. New York, NY Academy of Sciences, 2001.

3.   Arnold LE: Treatment alternatives for attention-deficit/hyperactivity disorder. In: Jensen PS, Cooper J, eds. *Diagnosis and Treatment of ADHD: An Evidence-Based Approach*. Washington, DC, APA Press, 2001. In press.

4.   Breakey J: The role of diet and behavior in childhood. *J Pediatr Child Health* 1997;33:190-194.

5.   Arnold LE, Votolato NA, Kleykamp D, et al: Does hair zinc predict amphetamine improvement of ADHD/Hyperactivity? *Int J Neurosci* 1990;50:103-107.

6.   Zhang H, Huang J: Preliminary study of traditional Chinese medicine treatment of minimal brain dysfunction: analysis of 100 cases. *Chung Hsi i Chieh Ho Tsa Chih (Chinese Journal of Modern Developments in Traditional Medicine)* 1990;10:278-279.

7.   Wang LH, Li CS, Li GZ: Clinical and experimental studies on tiaoshen liquor for infantile hyperkinetic syndrome. *Chung-Kuo Chung Hsi i Chieh Ho Tsa Chih* 1995;15:337-340.

8.   Zentall SS, Hall AM, Lee DL: Attentional focus of students with hyperactivity during a word-search task. *J Abnormal Child Psychol* 1998;26:335-343.

9.   Arnold LE: Some nontraditional (unconventional and/or innovative) psychosocial treatments for children and adolescents: critique and proposed screening principles. *J Abnorm Child Psychol* 1995;23:125-140.

10.   Field T, Lasko D, Mundy P, et al: Brief report: autistic children's attentiveness and responsivity improve after touch therapy. *J Autism Dev Disord* 1996;27:333-338.

11. Ironson G, Field T, Scafidi F, et al: Massage therapy is associated with enhancement of the immune system's cytotoxic capacity. *Int J Neurosci* 1996;84:205-217.

12. Field TM, Quintino O, Hernandez-Reif M, et al: Adolescents with attention-deficit/hyperactivity disorder benefit from massage therapy. *Adolescence* 1998;33:103-108.

13. Hagerman RJ, Falkenstein AR: An association between recurrent otitis media in infancy and hyperactivity. *Clin Pediatr* 1987;26:253-257.

14. Vargas SL, Patrick CC, Ayers GD, et al: Modulating effect of dietary carbohydrate supplementation on *Candida albicans* colonization and invasion in a neutropenic mouse model. *Infect Immun* 1993;61:619-626.

15. Truss CO: A controlled trial of nystatin for the candidiasis hypersensitivity syndrome (letter to editor). *N Engl J Med* 1991.

Chapter 8

Treatment Team for Chronic Care: Explaining ADHD

One of the key concepts in managing ADHD is understanding that it is a chronic, perhaps life-long, disorder that requires long-range planning.[1] This, in turn, requires forming a treatment team with staying power and organization for the long term. Clinicians are among those team members, but they are interchangeable, and, in the age of managed care, are indeed often changed. But patients and their caretakers or significant others are not interchangeable, so they need proper orientation and staying power for a long-term effort. Note that the first four team members listed in Table 8-1 are not clinicians. The American Academy of Pediatrics (AAP) 2001 Practice Guideline specifically recognizes the importance of these treatment team members and the communication among them.[1]

Clinicians who help manage ADHD patients can represent different disciplines, partly depending on the interests of the clinician. For example, medication might be managed by a primary care clinician, a psychiatrist, or a neurologist. Behavioral interventions and psychiatric comorbidity evaluations might be managed by a psychiatrist or psychologist, or perhaps by a psychiatric social worker or psychiatric nurse. Therefore, not all team clinicians need to be involved in every case. Chapter 10 addresses the indications for specialty referrals.

Table 8-1: Key Members of the Treatment Team for ADHD in Approximate Order of Importance

Team Member	Reason/Role
Patient	Ultimate responsibility; compliance with Tx
Parent (if patient is child)	Legal and practical responsibility; monitor and support compliance
Teacher (if patient is child); possibly counselor, school nurse, or principal if no identifiable primary teacher	Accurate direct information/ observations; cooperation with school aspect of Tx (administration of medication at school, daily report card, etc)
Significant other or work supervisor (if adult)	Communication, observation, compliance support (in lieu of parent and teacher)
Primary care clinician (physician or nurse practitioner)	Diagnosis of ADHD; medication management; diagnosis and Tx of related physical causes/problems; possibly supportive counseling; possibly simple behavioral interventions
Support group (family, CHADD, ADDA, church)	Additional resources; maintain morale; acceptance of patient

When children are treated, they are often overlooked as team members even though they are the ones who will be involved in treatment the longest and who will need to comply with management regimens later in life. Therefore, any

Team Member	Reason/Role
Psychiatrist	Diagnosis and management of ADHD and comborbid psychiatric disorders; medication management; behavioral interventions
Psychologist (school or private)	Psychoeducational or neuropsychologic assessment; refined behavioral interventions; diagnosis of psychiatric disorders
Neurologist (if indicated)	Consult on neurologic problems; possible seizures: diagnosis and management
Other consultants and specialty referrals as indicated (allergist, endocrinologist, occupational therapist, physiatrist, physical therapist, social worker)	Diagnosis/Tx of more complicated physical causes or comorbidity; provision of specialized treatment or supportive services (eg, for food sensitivity, thyroid dysfunction, incoordination, disorganized family)

management strategy must devote some effort to ensuring collaboration with the patient, the most important person on the treatment team (Table 8-2). To this end, it is important that the patient and family have a clear understanding of the disorder.

**Table 8-2: Strategies and Tactics for
Eliciting and Cementing the
Cooperation of a Child Patient
in the Treatment of ADHD**

Strategy/Tactic	Rationale, Purpose
Speak directly to a child in explaining the disorder and the treatment; let the parent get information by listening in.	Shows respect for child, makes child active team member. Child will appreciate and parent won't mind.
Check the child's understanding of the explanation; ask if any questions.	Shows the clinician cares and takes the child's role seriously. If not understood, confusion can be cleared up.
Ask the child's agreement with the treatment plan.	Ultimately, the plan's success depends on the child's cooperation. The worst that can happen is a negative response; better to have it verbalized at the beginning than passively-aggressively expressed.
Assume that if child resists treatment, especially medication, there is a good reason, and that reason should be addressed.	Sometimes the child has a good reason, such as not wanting to take medicine at school because peers would know, or the taste is objectionable. Usually, the reason can be resolved, and doing so cements the rapport.
If child resists adamantly, ask cooperation 'under protest.'	Implies the child is a good sport who will play the game even if he or she disagrees with the umpire. Provides face-saving way to cooperate.
See the child alone for a few minutes at each visit to see if there is anything he or she wishes to say confidentially.	Shows respect for privacy. Child will often disclose problems with compliance that parent was unaware of or downplayed.

How to Explain ADHD

The points to be made in explaining ADHD and its treatment options are listed in Table 8-3. Additional background information can be found in Chapters 1 and 2. The following explanation is an example and is not meant to be a script for universal application; in this example, the patient is a 9-year-old boy (the most common age group of diagnosis is elementary school), but a similar explanation could be made to adolescents and adults, with obvious age-related changes. Younger children require some language simplification. For preschoolers, most of the explanation after the beginning is addressed to the parents. This is done with the child and parents together:

Sample Explanation

"Well, Joe, you've given me a lot of information, as have your parents and teacher, so now I'd like to tell you my understanding of your problems, and then we can figure out what to do about them. I think you already know some of this. For example, when you first came in and I asked why you were here, you said 'I'm hyper' and explained that means you keep pacing around the classroom, can't sit still, and lose your temper easily. That's a pretty good description of two of the main problems in attention-deficit/hyperactivity disorder, called ADHD for short. Other names sometimes used for this diagnosis are ADD (just plain attention-deficit disorder) and hyperactivity or hyperkinesis (sometimes abbreviated to 'hyper'). Don't worry about all the names; I just mentioned them in case you ever hear them.

"ADHD has three main symptoms, first, attention problems—having trouble concentrating, not being able to finish work, forgetting things, having trouble getting organized, and so forth; second, hyperactivity or overactivity, which you called 'hyper'; and third, impulsiveness—acting or speaking before you think. Other symptoms include being fussy—losing your temper easily, which you mentioned—and restless sleep, which your mother mentioned.

159

Table 8-3: Points for Explanation and Clarification to Patient and Family

Talking Point	Reason
Acknowledge what they already know.	Shows respect and attention to their story. Imparts feeling of cognitive familiarity, a base on which to hook the new information.
Give them the current name of the disorder, indicating there are numerous other names.	Defines and clarifies the disorder.
ADHD has many symptoms, and not every patient with ADHD has all of them. Some have partial expressions of the syndrome.	Prevents confusion from having symptoms that are different from those of an acquaintance with ADHD.
Three main symptoms are inattention, hyperactivity, and impulsivity.	Focuses the targets of treatment. Prevents assumption the patient needs to be aggressive.
Other symptoms are frequent and often disabling, though not important for the diagnosis.	Puts all symptoms in perspective.

Talking Point	Reason
Symptoms are just excess amounts of normal behavior.	Implies need to control symptoms, not eliminate them
Symptoms are not the patient's fault, but the patient can improve with help.	Breaks up the blame game, prevents giving up. Promotes teamwork in fighting ADHD.
ADHD lasts a long time, perhaps a lifetime, although it tends to get better with age.	Prepares for long-term treatment.
Important not to give up or neglect treatment.	Giving up allows secondary problems, dropping farther behind.
Treatment helps prevent secondary problems.	So they don't just wait for things to get better.
Many different treatments are available, relative advantages/ disadvantages, and scientific basis of each (Chapters 3 to 7).	So they'll know the options, be involved in choice of treatment, and, therefore, commit to it.

In addition to the hyperactivity and impulsiveness that you and your mother described, your teacher noticed attention problems. Those are the three main symptoms of ADHD. Of course, other things can cause these symptoms besides ADHD, and that's why I asked how you feel, what you worry about, and what you are afraid of, to make sure sadness or anxiety are not causing them.

"You've had these symptoms for as far back as your mother can remember, which also fits ADHD, because it's a long-lasting problem. The good news is that it seems to get a little better with time, especially with treatment. The bad news is that in some cases it never completely leaves. However, even when it doesn't completely leave, it can get better and you can learn to live with it and make up for it in other ways. Also, with treatment and other help, you can prevent the secondary problems, the additional problems that ADHD tends to cause if untreated. If you quit trying to get better, you would fall farther behind and things would get much worse because you'd let the secondary problems creep in, and sometimes they're worse than the ADHD."

To the parents: "In fact, one of the main goals of treatment is to prevent secondary discouragement, depression, underachievement, school drop-out, accidents, and delinquency."

Then return to child: "That's why it's important to keep working and plugging away. If you do keep at it, things will gradually get better." (At this point, mention some strength of the child that he or she can draw on. For example:) "Because you're smart you'll be able to figure out some things to help yourself." Or: "Because you are a hard worker and so determined, that will help you overcome some of the problems."

"It's important for you—and your parents—(smiling momentarily towards the parents) to realize that it's not your fault that you have these symptoms. Studies have shown that it's something about the way your brain is working, maybe something you were born with. But that doesn't mean you can't do something to help it. Some people are natural-born swimmers; they quickly learn without taking lessons. But others have to take lessons to learn and some need more lessons than others. The ones who have to take lessons might get to be better swimmers than the natural swimmers if they work at it and practice. In the same way, some kids just naturally pay attention and calmly control their impulses, but other kids have to practice paying attention, being calm, and controlling impulses. You're one of the kids who needs to take lessons and practice. And it won't be instant success; it's something you'll have to work at for years. Do you think you can do that?"

This kind of explanation, with an invitation to ask questions, is as much for the parents as for the child, but it is best directed to the child (except for preschoolers). For adolescents (and adults), it becomes critical to direct it to the patient.

Additional family members may also need education. For example, a sibling may be embarrassed about the patient's behavior or may blame the patient for a moral failing. A grandparent may take a blaming attitude toward the child and the parents (for 'not disciplining' adequately). Interrupting the blaming cycle by education about the disorder is, in fact, one of the strategies for breaking up the vicious cycles depicted in Figure 3-1.

Other Team Members

The teacher or other school contact personnel should be contacted directly at least once to establish a working relationship. In addition to teacher cooperation through such interventions as a daily report card (Chapter 6), regular feedback needs to come from the school by e-mail, phone, fax, rating forms, or other written information sent with the family at each visit. Trying to manage a child's ADHD medication without direct teacher information is like trying to manage diabetes without obtaining blood sugar levels. It is not unusual for parents to report that a given medication is seemingly ineffective, while the teacher notes amazing improvement. Both observations may be valid because the parents typically see the child only after the dose wears off and not in the demanding academic setting of school, where the medication makes a difference. The child's behavior and performance can vary by setting and activity, as well as by time from dose administration. Hence, using observations from as many settings as possible is important.

In modern times, the relevant settings may include after-school 'latchkey' or day-care programs, so it may be useful to obtain ratings or other information from the directors of those programs or from informal sitters. In some cases, sitters or day-care providers can be recruited to perform behavioral interventions, such as a report card or token economy. Other potential sources of information include coaches, Scout leaders, and other adults in the community.

Many teachers are now aware of ADHD as a disorder, although they sometimes need clarifications, but other nonclinical care providers may need more education about ADHD to be supportive and cooperate with communicating observations. Again, an important point to publicize is the fact that ADHD is a chronic disorder with the potential for gradual improvement.

Metropolitan areas and many medium-sized communities have a chapter of Children and Adults With Attention-Deficit/Hyperactivity Disorder (CHADD), or the National Attention Deficit Disorder Association (ADDA), or other support organizations. Although they are self-help support groups, they cooperate with professional efforts. Parents who feel overwhelmed by their child's problems or adult patients who feel alone may benefit from referral to such a group, which may be considered part of the treatment team in promoting compliance and consistent efforts.

Clinical Team Members

Clinical members of the treatment team should develop some means of routine communication, such as sharing progress notes or sending a note with the patient or family. If the clinical team members are in the same clinic, a periodic meeting might be better to go over their joint cases. The first clinician to be involved should make sure that all indicated disciplines are accessed, making referrals as needed. In particular, the primary clinician needs to think about referrals to the disciplines listed in the last row of Table 8-1, when such referrals are indicated.

References

1.   Clinical practice guideline: treatment of the school-aged child with attention-deficit/hyperactivity disorder. *Pediatrics* 2001;108:1033-1044.

Chapter 9

Age Considerations in ADHD

Since the first report of a 'hyperkinetic' adult[1] in 1972, clinical awareness has increased that ADHD does not always vanish with puberty. As children with ADHD age, some attenuation of symptoms occurs, especially overactivity, but significant numbers of patients continue to meet diagnostic criteria into adulthood. Also, some older patients who no longer meet diagnostic criteria suffer residual subclinical impairment, especially in attention, organization, impulse control, and other executive functions (Figure 9-1). Thus, ADHD is a chronic disorder, perhaps lifelong. Both diagnosis and treatment are affected by the patient's age.

Age Considerations in Diagnostic Evaluation

Diagnostically, age (and mental age) peer comparisons, both quantitative and qualitative, must be used in deciding whether the patient's symptoms reach a pathologic level. A degree of fidgeting, excessive locomotor activity, distractibility, and impulsiveness that would be considered within the normal range for a 4-year-old, or even a 7-year-old, would be excessive for a 25-year-old. Qualitatively, the symptoms may be expressed differently[2,3] (Table 9-1). While the 7-year-old might show observable squirming, fidgeting, and locomotor hyperactivity, the

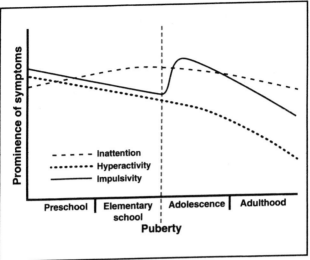

Figure 9-1: *Relative changes in prominence of primary ADHD symptom clusters with age (based on clinical experience and literature, not hard data). Under the influence of pubertal hormones, impulsiveness may show a temporary blip in its general tendency to abate with maturity. Hyperactivity shows a more consistent decline with age, while inattentiveness/disorganization may be the most persistent.*

adolescent or adult may merely feel restless while sitting still. While impulsiveness in the 7-year-old may manifest as blurting out answers or physical aggression when frustrated, the adolescent or adult may jump to conclusions, drive a vehicle impulsively, or abruptly quit a job when frustrated. While the 7-year-old's inattentiveness and disorganization may manifest as misplaced homework, failure to complete tasks, or forgetting chores, an adult may forget appointments or have difficulty with details on a work project.

The relative importance of the primary symptoms also tends to vary with age: hyperactivity tends to become less

Table 9-1: Age-specific Manifestations of ADHD

Primary symptomatology and prominent comorbidities are often age-based in ADHD patients.[2,3] Here are

	Attention Problems	Hyperactivity
Preschool age	Difficulty finishing mental-age-appropriate puzzles or games, listening until end of age-appropriate story, or finishing age-appropriate video. Careless accidents.	Constant running; climbs bookshelves, etc. Breaks or wears out toys. Runs away. Can't sit through meal, spills things. Restless sleep.
Elementary school	Difficulty finishing schoolwork, homework, chores. Failure to follow instructions. Difficulty with group work/instruction. Loses things. Forgetful, disorganized. Distractable.	Difficulty sitting still; squirms and fidgets; taps, hums, fiddles with things. Flits from one thing to another. Wears out friends. 'Immature.'
Adolescence	Disorganized, overwhelmed by independent responsibilities for middle, high school. Missing assignments. Forgets chores, instructions. Bored. Accident-prone.	Restless feeling. Jittery, often moving body part. Often in the wrong place at the wrong time. 'On the go' as much as possible.
Adulthood	Needs frequent breaks, forgets appointments, deadlines. Difficulty organizing, planning. Undependable, may not finish projects. Misjudges time. Can't concentrate.	Restless feeling. May pace when acceptable; frequent trips to water cooler, coffee station, or restroom.

generalizations for a conceptual picture, but many individual case exceptions will be encountered.

Impulsivity	Comorbidity
Trouble waiting turn or for meal, treat. Darts off in public places. Impatient, demanding, short temper, perhaps aggressive, destructive. Tantrums. Gets in dangerous situations. Interrupts.	Oppositional-defiant disorder (ODD), anxiety. Argumentative.
Blurts answers before question finished, jumps to conclusions, difficulty waiting turn in games or recitation. Loses friends by inconsiderate impulsiveness. Intrudes, interrupts.	50% ODD or conduct disorder, 33% anxiety disorder, 20%+ learning disorder; some mood disorder, some tics.
Earlier and more severe experimentation with sex, drugs. Changes job, maybe friends frequently. Accident prone. Drives erratically. May drop out of school. Delinquency.	50% ODD or conduct disorder. More mood disorder after puberty. Some learning disorder. Poor self-esteem. Poor peer relations. Difficulty with authority.
Quits job easily. Spends impulsively. Marital problems. Novelty seeking. Changes of significant other. Poor anger control. Misdemeanors.	Mood disorder, 10% to 40% substance abuse, 10% to 25% personality disorder, 30% to 50% anxiety disorder.

Table 9-2: Age-specific Effectiveness of Treatments/Interventions

Comparisons should be made only across rows, not down columns; eg, meditation for adults is not necessarily better than stimulants for adults, but is

	Preschool
Stimulants	+++
Antidepressants	+++
Self-administered behavioral Tx	0
Behavioral Tx via others	++++
Elimination diets	++++
Perceptual training/stimulation	++++
Relaxation training/ EMG biofeedback	+
Meditation	0
Repletion of deficiency states	++++
Change of workplace (classroom, job, day care)	+++

Key:

++++ = as effective at this age as at any

  +++ = very effective, but less than at other ages

    ++ = effective, but definitely less effective than at other ages

prominent, while attentional problems persist and impulsiveness may lead to increasingly serious secondary problems (Figure 9-1). The type of comorbidity that is most prominent can also vary with age[4-7] (Table 9-1).

better than meditation for preschoolers. The lower half of this list has a dramatically decreasing data base from which to derive estimates.

Elementary School	Adolescence	Adulthood
++++	+++	+++
+++	++++	++++
++	+++	++++
++++	+++	+
++	+	+
++++	++	+
+++	++++	++++
+++	++++	++++
++++	+	+
++	++	++++

+ = little or no scientific evidence of effect at this age, but probably some effect

0 = no evidence of effect at this age, or it seems unlikely

Age Considerations in Treatment

Although many medications (eg, stimulants, antidepressants) have demonstrated efficacy throughout the life span, their effectiveness can vary with age, and some treatments have definite age limitations (Table 9-2). Many patients who fail to respond to a stimulant as preschoolers later respond during elementary school.[8-10] Antidepressants seem to have increasing utility with older age. In contrast, the best candidates for elimination diet are preschoolers.

Choice of behavioral treatments is even more affected by a patient's age. Young children generally need behavioral intervention structured by others; hence, the importance of parent training, teacher consultation, and a daily report card. On the other hand, adults, for whom parent training would be ludicrous, may be able to carry out a self-administered behavioral program with appropriate coaching.

Another intervention possible for an adult but not feasible for a child is a change of occupation. It may be feasible for an adult to switch jobs or occupations to something more compatible with ADHD. For example, the first adult diagnosed with ADHD[1] worked as an accountant, where he sat at a desk in one of several rows in a large room without partitions between desks. He continually got in trouble with his supervisor for wandering around and making frequent trips to the water cooler. After a recommendation to consider a different kind of work, he switched to a sales job, where his energetic, outgoing personality served him well. An important point is that he did not think of switching jobs until the clinician raised the issue.

Thus, in thinking creatively about an individual patient's treatment plan, age is an important consideration for feasibility and likely effectiveness. In fact, a reason for re-evaluating and modifying the treatment plan periodically (as recommended by the American Academy of Pediatrics [AAP] 2001 Guideline) is to adjust for age effects.[11] Another is that patients and their circumstances change over time. Of course, individual variations and exceptions occur to the average, expected course of the disorder. Thus, the patient's developmental trajectory must be addressed in a well-monitored treatment plan.

References

1. Arnold LE, Strobl D, Weisenberg A: Hyperkinetic adult: study of the paradoxical amphetamine response. *JAMA* 1972;222:693-694.

2. Conners CK, Jett JL: *Attention-Deficit/Hyperactivity Disorder (in Adults and Children)*. Kansas City, MO, Compact Clinicals, 1999.

3. Greenhill LL: Diagnosing attention-deficit/hyperactivity disorder in children. *J Clin Psychiatry* 1998;59(suppl 7):31-41.

4. Biederman J, Faraone SV, Spencer T, et al: Patterns of psychiatric comorbidity, cognition, and psychosocial functioning in adults with attention-deficit/hyperactivity disorder. *Am J. Psychiatry* 1993;150:1792-1798.

5. Pliszka SR: Comorbidity of attention-deficit/hyperactivity disorder: an overview. *J Clin Psychiatry* 1998;59(suppl 7):50-58.

6. Spencer T, Biederman J, Wilens TE, et al: Adults with attention-deficit/hyperactivity disorder: a controversial diagnosis. *J Clin Psychiatry* 1998;59(suppl 7):59-68.

7. Hornig M: Addressing comorbidity in adults with attention-deficit/hyperactivity disorder. *J Clin Psychiatry* 1998;59(suppl 7):69-75.

8. Conners CK: Controlled trial of methylphenidate in preschool children with minimal brain dysfunction. In: Gittelman R, Klein, eds. *Recent Advances in Child Psychopharmacology*. New York, Human Sciences Press, 1975.

9. Schleifer M, Weiss G, Cohen NJ, et al: Hyperactivity in preschoolers and the effect of methylphenidate. *Am J Orthopsychiatry* 1975;45:38-50.

10. Cohen NJ, Sullivan J, Minde K, et al: Evaluation of the relative effectiveness of methylphenidate and cognitive behavior modification in the treatment of kindergarten-aged hyperactive children. *J Abnorm Child Psychol* 1981;9:43-54.

11. Clinical practice guideline: treatment of the school-aged child with attention-deficit/hyperactivity disorder. *Pediatrics* 2001;108:1033-1044.

Chapter 10

When, How, and Why to Refer to or Consult With a Specialist

Many uncomplicated cases of ADHD, especially those occurring in intact, well-functioning families, can be effectively managed by a primary care physician (PCP) who is willing to take the time to properly monitor treatment, especially the careful titration and regular communication needed for optimal medication. In some cases, however, consultation with a specialist is useful, and in still others, referral to a specialist for treatment is advisable (Table 10-1). To optimize results, the primary care physician should decide clearly whether he or she wishes the specialist to evaluate and diagnose, to make recommendations based on an established diagnosis, to assume management within a restricted area (such as seizures, allergy, or need for supplementary behavioral treatment), to assume total management, or to decide whether the case requires specialist management. Integration of services with other specialists is recommended by the American Academy of Pediatrics (AAP) 2001 Guideline.[1]

When To Refer or Consult

A basic rule is that a consultation or referral to a specialist should be sought any time the primary care physician feels uncomfortable with a case, its diagnosis, its treatment planning, or the patient's response to treatment. In the extreme case, this means that any primary care physician who does not want to treat ADHD, or is unable to devote the necessary time for titration and monitoring of dose, time-action effects, side effects, and teacher observations, could appropriately refer all cases to a clinician who has the time and interest for it, whether a specialist or another primary care physician. In some cases, a primary care physician may feel comfortable attempting initial treatment but later refer to a specialist if complications or comorbidity become evident, if treatment results are unsatisfactory, or if the case becomes unusual in any other way.

To Whom To Refer

Table 10-1 summarizes suggested specialists for given situations. The overlapping expertise of psychiatrists and neurologists deserves comment. These two specialties have the same board (American Board of Psychiatry and Neurology), with different but partly overlapping examinations. The division of labor has many unclear borders, but, generally, neurologists have traditionally focused more on gross motor and sensory abnormalities, gross CNS lesions, seizures, traumatic injuries, infections, toxicology, etc. Psychiatrists have focused more on disorders of mood, affect, cognition, behavior, and social adaptation—disorders of the psychobiologic unit. With increasing knowledge, neurobiologic bases are being discovered for nearly all psychiatric disorders (as Freud predicted a century ago), so that the interests and expertise of the two specialties are converging. ADHD and Tourette's syndrome are two disorders where the shared interest is evident. Both specialties are competent in the diagnosis and medical management of these disorders; but most psychiatrists can also provide psychosocial treatments such as behavior therapy, family therapy, and

Table 10-1: When to Refer to or Consult With a Specialist for ADHD

Situation or Complication	Referral (R) or Consultation (C)	For
Question of psychiatric comorbidity or unusual presentation of ADHD	Psychiatrist, psychologist, or other licensed mental health professional (C)	Psychiatric diagnostic evaluation
Confirmed psychiatric comorbidity or other complication that the PCP feels comfortable managing	Psychiatrist (C)	Consultation about treatment plan
Confirmed psychiatric comorbidity that the PCP does not feel comfortable managing	Psychiatrist (R)	Treatment management
A degree of ADHD severity that requires more intense or expert management than the PCP can provide	Psychiatrist or developmental/behavioral pediatrician (R)	Treatment management

PCP = primary care physician

Situation or Complication	Referral (R) or Consultation (C)	For
Confirmed psychiatric comorbidity or degree of ADHD severity for which the PCP feels able to manage the medication but not supplementary Tx	Psychologist, psychiatrist, psychiatric social worker (SW), psychiatric nurse (R)	Psychotherapy, behavioral Tx, family therapy, psycho-education, etc.
	Psychiatrist (C)	Consultation on medication management
Suspected seizure disorder or other neurologic comorbidity or complication	Neurologist (C or R)	Neurologic diagnostic evaluation and treatment recommendations
Confirmed seizure disorder or other neurologic co-morbidity that the PCP feels comfortable managing	Neurologist (C)	Consultation on treatment plan and interaction of ADHD and seizure medications
Confirmed seizure disorder or other neurologic comorbidity that the PCP feels unable to manage	Neurologist (R)	Management of neurologic disorder or of both ADHD and neurologic disorder

(continued on next page)

Table 10-1: When to Refer to or Consult With a Specialist for ADHD
(continued)

Situation or Complication	Referral (R) or Consultation (C)	For
Suspected learning disorder	Psychologist (may often be arranged free through school), behavioral pediatric clinic* (C or R)	Psycho-educational testing; diagnostic evaluation and recommenda-tions
Confirmed learning disorder	Special educational services of the school; private tutors; supple-mentary learning centers (R)	Remedial classes, re-source rooms, structured activities
Developmental coordination disorder	Behavioral/ developmental pediatrician, physiatrist occupational therapist, physical therapist, adaptive physical education (R)	Assessment and Tx plan; graduated motor skill practice; sensorimotor integration; success experiences at ability level

* Behavioral pediatric clinics often have psychologists avail-able. See text.

Situation or Complication	Referral (R) or Consultation (C)	For
Family unwilling to use medication	Psychologist, psychiatrist, psychiatric SW, psychiatric nurse skilled in behavioral Tx (R)	Intensive, comprehensive behavioral intervention
Thyroid or other endocrine abnormality	Endocrinologist (C or R)	Treatment recommendations or management for endocrine problem; management of both ADHD and endocrine problem if intimately linked
Question of atopy, food sensitivities, or other allergies	Allergist (C or R)	Allergy evaluation and any indicated desensitization, recommendations about allergens to be avoided
Lead levels above 10 µg/dL	Toxicologist (C or R)	Recommendations about or supervision of chelation or other intervention as indicated

(continued on next page)

Table 10-1: When to Refer to or Consult With a Specialist for ADHD
(continued)

Situation or Complication	Referral (R) or Consultation (C)	For
Patient's response to treatment is unsatisfactory or puzzling	Psychiatrist, neurologist, or behavioral/ developmental pediatrician (C or R)	Diagnostic re-evaluation, adapted treatment plan, possible assumption of management at request of PCP
Adult patient has child with suspected ADHD and PCP does not treat children	Child psychiatrist, behavioral/ developmental pediatrician, child neurologist, child's regular physician (R)	Evaluation and any indicated management
Child patient has parent with suspected ADHD and PCP does not treat adults	Psychiatrist, neurologist, internist, family practitioner, parents' regular physician (R)	Evaluation and any indicated management

PCP = primary care physician

psychotherapy, whereas neurologists have more expertise in management of comorbid seizures and other neurologic complications.

An overlap also exists between psychiatry and psychology. Practitioners in both disciplines are competent in evaluation and diagnosis of mental, emotional, and behavioral disorders. Both are expert in psychodynamics. To some extent, both can provide psychosocial treatments. However, psychiatrists, because they are physicians, can also prescribe and recommend pharmacotherapy and other somatic treatments. Psychologists generally have more expertise in testing and in psychosocial treatments, such as behavior therapy, although the latter difference varies much by individual psychologist or psychiatrist.

Table 10-1 may be somewhat optimistic in describing what to expect from each specialist. The referral is complicated by the fact that for ADHD, not all specialists of a given discipline have expertise or interest in the same services (Table 10-2). For example, not all psychiatrists provide behavioral treatment (not even all psychologists). Not all allergists provide enzyme-potentiated desensitization; for that matter, not all take seriously the effect of food sensitivities on behavior, despite the placebo-controlled studies. Not all social workers are skilled in diagnosis of psychiatric comorbidity.

Therefore, the referring clinician must know something about the specific persuasion of the specialist to make an intelligent referral. If the clinician is not already familiar with who does what in the community, a few telephone calls can usually elicit the information. The following sources may be able to supply such information: the school system's special education department; community mental health clinics; and university departments of psychiatry, psychology, social work, and pediatrics.

Referral for psychoeducational testing for learning disorders poses an economic choice for the parents: By law, the school must provide indicated testing for suspected learning

Table 10-2: Areas of Expertise Within a Specialty

Not all specialists within a given discipline will have expertise, skill, or experience with all aspects of ADHD diagnosis and treatment.

Specialty	Consistent Skills/Expertise
Psychiatry	Diagnosis, psychopharmacology, psychodynamics For child psychiatrists: parent guidance
Neurology	Diagnosis, psychopharmacology, seizures, gross neurologic pathology
Psychology	Psychoeducational testing, diagnosis, behavior therapy, psychodynamics For child psychologists: parent guidance
Developmental/behavioral pediatrics	Diagnosis, psychopharmacology of ADHD, at least the main drugs
Allergy/immunology	Diagnosis and treatment of frank allergies, skin testing
Endocrinology	Diagnosis and management of thyroid or other endocrine abnormality

disorders, and insurance often does not cover it. However, the backlog for most school psychologists is so long that some parents choose to pay for private testing to expedite special education services. Child psychiatry and developmental/behavioral pediatric clinics usually have a psychologist available who can do the testing. The cli-

Variable According to Interest

Behavior therapy, family therapy
Some general (adult) psychiatrists may not treat patients
with ADHD.

Psychodynamics; rarely, behavior therapy
Some neurologists may not treat patients with ADHD

Projective testing, neuropsychologic testing,
family therapy
Some adult psychologists may not see patients
with ADHD

Diagnosis and psychopharmacology of comorbid
disorders, less common pharmacology of ADHD

Diagnosis and management of food sensitivities not
showing up on skin test
Enzyme-potentiated desensitization

Management of secondary behavioral problems rarely

nician needs to make sure the parents know their options
and the child's rights.

Specialists' Response

When receiving a referral, the specialist needs to determine the expectation of the primary care physician: is

Table 10-3: Appropriate Services by Specialists

Specialist	Referred From
Psychiatrist	Family practitioner, internist, pediatrician, or licensed nurse practitioner
	Neurologist
	Endocrinologist, allergist, other medical/surgical specialist
	Psychologist, social worker, or other mental health professional
Neurologist	Family practitioner, internist, pediatrician, or licensed nurse practitioner
	Psychiatrist
	Psychologist, social worker, or other mental health professional

Appropriate Services/Responses

Refined diagnostic evaluation; diagnosis of comorbidity; assessment of impairment/severity; psychopharmacologic recommendations; provision of adjunctive psychosocial treatment; assumption of comorbidity management or of total management on request of referring clinician; offer of ongoing consultation if case seems manageable by referring clinician but requires reevaluation periodically; offer to assume management (perhaps temporarily) if case seems too complicated or severe for consultative disposal.

Comorbidity evaluation; provision of adjunctive psychosocial treatment; psychopharmacologic recommendations about comorbidity; assumption of management on request of referring neurologist.

Evaluation and diagnosis; ongoing consultation/recommendations vs assumption of management, according to request of referring specialist and needs of the patient.

Confirmation of diagnosis (ADHD and comorbidity); management of any indicated psychopharmacology; recommendations about psychosocial treatment if requested/appropriate.

Diagnostic evaluation; ruling out of neurologic mimic, seizures, other neurologic disorder; pharmacologic recommendations; assumption of seizure management or total management at request of referring clinician

Neurologic evaluation; ruling out of seizures, other neurologic disorder; recommendations about treatment of any neurologic comorbidity; assumption of seizure management or total management at request of referring psychiatrist.

Neurologic evaluation; ruling out of seizures, other neurologic disorder; management of any indicated psychopharmacology (or referral to another appropriate physician).

(continued on next page)

185

Table 10-3: Appropriate Services by Specialists (continued)

Specialist	Referred From
Psychologist	Family practitioner, internist, pediatrician, or licensed nurse practitioner
	Psychiatrist
	Endocrinologist, allergist, other medical/ surgical specialty
Developmental/ behavioral pediatrician	Family practitioner, general pediatrician, or licensed nurse practitioner
	Psychiatrist
	Psychologist
	Non-mental health specialist

this a request mainly for diagnostic confirmation and consultative recommendations, or a request to assume management? If the former, is there a specific question? If the latter, is the request to assume total management or just one part, such as the psychosocial treatment? Or is

Appropriate Services/Responses

Diagnostic evaluation, including comorbidity; any indicated psychological testing; recommendation and provision of any indicated psychosocial treatment.

Any indicated psychological testing; provision of behavioral or other psychosocial treatment as requested by referring psychiatrist.

Diagnostic evaluation and recommendations about treatment plan and additional referrals; assumption of management within area of expertise on request, referring to appropriate physician if medication indicated.

Diagnostic evaluation; pharmacotherapy recommendations; appropriate additional referral recommendations; assumption of management on request of referring clinician.

Physical and general health evaluation; management of med/surg problems.

Physical and general health evaluation; management of any indicated pharmacotherapy.

Diagnostic evaluation; recommendations; assumption of managment on request of referring clinician.

the referring clinician unsure and wants the specialist to decide who should manage the case? In some cases, the answer may be implied by the respective disciplines of the two clinicians. Table 10-3 shows some useful responses by specialists to various referring clinicians.

References

1.   Clinical practice guideline: treatment of the school-aged child with attention-deficit/hyperactivity disorder. *Pediatrics* 2001;108:1033-1044.

Index

A

academic performance 64

acetaminophen 116

acetylcholine 140

acupuncture 61

Adderall® 77, 78, 83, 89, 90, 93, 110, 118, 120

addiction 97, 113

aggression 18, 20, 21, 69, 84, 90, 142

agitation 45, 47, 87

α_2-agonists 60, 68, 69, 77, 80, 86, 115

β-agonists 52

akathisia 87

alcohol 22

allergist 179, 181, 184, 186

allergy 50, 174

American Academy of Pediatrics (AAP) 2001 Practice Guideline 30, 31, 43, 59, 60, 61, 63, 64, 77, 107, 109, 111, 155

American Board of Psychiatry and Neurology 175

American Psychiatric Association 30
Diagnostic and Statistical Manual (DSM) 7, 12, 30, 31, 34
DSM-IV 8, 9, 18, 33, 37

American Psychiatric Press, Inc. 40

amino acid supplementation 140

amitriptyline (Endep®, Elavil®) 79, 80

amphetamine (Adderall®, Benzedrine®) 42, 71, 77-79, 83, 88-90, 98, 115, 117

Anafranil® 79

anergia 44, 52

anger 47

anorexia 46, 88, 90

anticonvulsants 42, 52, 71, 80

antidepressants 60, 68, 71, 77, 80, 87, 94, 95, 111, 140, 149, 170, 171

antifungal treatment 152

antihistamines 50, 86

antisocial behavior 43

dry skin 52
dyscrasia 87

E

eczema 50
EFA metabolism 140
Effexor® 79
Elavil® 79
electrocardiogram 96
electroencephalogram (EEG) 41, 42
electroencephalographic (EEG) biofeedback 61, 142, 149
electromyographic (EMG) biofeedback 61, 150, 170
encephalitis 14
Endep® 79
endocrinologist 179, 184, 186
enzyme-potentiated desensitization 140, 147, 181, 183
eosinophilia 140
essential fatty acids 61, 140, 148
Eutonyl® 79
evening crash 85
excitation 87
explosiveness 86
extortion 48

F

family practitioner 186
family response 64
family therapy 183
fantasy 47
fatigue 44, 46, 52
fatty acids 14, 52
fidgeting 17, 44, 168
fighting 48
flapping 45
flightiness 44
fluoxetine (Prozac®) 79, 81
Focalin™ 77, 78, 83, 89
Food and Drug Administration (FDA) 68, 80, 81, 92, 98
food sensitivity 16, 50, 51, 181, 183
forgetfulness 8, 44

G

glyconutritional supplementation 140, 148
grandiosity 44
growth suppression 89
guanfacine (Tenex®) 80, 96, 100, 101

neuropathy 142

neurotoxicity 96, 140

nicotine 22, 97

nicotine patch 97

NIMH Multimodal Treatment Study of ADHD (MTA) 106, 107, 136

Norpramin® 79, 95

nortriptyline (Pamelor®) 79, 98

nurse practitioner 184, 186

O

obsessive-compulsive disorder 52

occupational therapist 178

oppositional disorder 70

oppositional-aggressive behavior 106

oppositional-defiant disorder (ODD) 20, 21, 43, 48, 69, 113, 169

overactivity 5, 8, 58, 84, 111, 159

P

pacing 45

palpitations 47

Pamelor® 79

panic 45

pargyline (Eutonyl®) 79

Parnate® 79

parsnips 148

pediatric autoimmune neuropsychiatric disorder associated with group A *Streptococcus* (PANDAS) 151

pediatrician 178, 180, 184, 186

pemoline (Cylert®) 77, 78, 84, 96, 117

pepper 148

perfectionism 45, 47

performance test 88

personality disorder 12

Pertofrane® 79

pharyngitis 57

phenylalanine 82

phenytoin (Dilantin®) 80

phobias 21, 43, 47

physiatrist 178

physical therapist 178

placebo effect 107, 110

positron emission tomography (PET) 14

potatoes 148

poverty 70

preverbal child 42

primary care physician (PCP) 32, 174, 175, 177

propranolol (Inderal®) 82

Notes

Notes

Notes

Notes

Notes

Notes

Notes

Notes

Notes